THE BIGGEST LOSER

SECRETS OF OUR SUCCESS

EBURY
PRESS

Contents

The Biggest Loser Secrets and Strategies Unveiled!

Your health is your most valuable asset. Beyond looking attractive, the advantages of staying in shape are increased levels of stamina, a heightened sense of wellbeing, and a joy and confidence that shine from within. Who wouldn't want all that?

The great news is it doesn't matter what shape you are now – the power to transform your body and your life is in your hands! As *The Biggest Loser* illustrates, dramatic and permanent weight loss *is* possible and can be achieved by anyone. If you have ever dreamed of living a better life and creating a healthy and happy future for yourself, then this book is for you!

On the following pages you will meet contestants from every season of *The Biggest Loser* who have created exciting new destinies for themselves. These are people who have weighed more than 100, 150 or even 200 kilograms, but who have successfully changed their exercise, eating and thinking habits forever.

Now in its fourth season, *The Biggest Loser* has not only documented the contestants' outer transformations but also their inner journeys and the struggles they have faced. If you have seen the show you will have witnessed these women and men weighing in every week, battling the scales and defying the odds by losing a quarter, a third or even half their body weight.

But exactly how did they take themselves from fat to fab and go on to lead vibrantly fit and healthy lives?

In this book, the contestants reveal the secrets of their success, offering valuable tips and insights. They share their experiences and strategies for staying in shape while living back in the real world and facing everyday situations and temptations.

The Biggest Loser expert trainers Shannan and Michelle are also on hand to provide both practical and psychological pointers for losing weight and keeping it off, as well as helping you stay motivated along the way.

The Biggest Loser has helped many people claim the body and destiny they deserve, and now it's your turn. As you are about to see, *The Biggest Loser: Secrets of Our Success* is not just a guide for weight loss, it's a way of life!

It *is* possible to create the body you desire and the life of your dreams. With the right information, expert help and a determination to succeed, an exciting new future is yours for the taking.

Michelle Bridges: Fitness Professional and Celebrity Trainer

Having worked in the fitness industry for over 17 years, and a regular presenter at both a national and international level, Michelle Bridges was a natural choice as a trainer on *The Biggest Loser*.

'I have loved sports and training from a very young age,' she says. 'I was teaching fitness classes at fourteen and was awarded my training qualifications by the time I was eighteen.' An avid sportsperson and committed athlete, Michelle advocates living a healthy lifestyle every single day. 'Keeping fit is a daily decision. Every day I wake up and ask myself what I am going to do in terms of exercise and nutrition.

'I preach the value of consistency. You need to be making the smart choices constantly to reap the benefits. Research indicates that if you eat right and train regularly – that is, most days of the week – it is almost impossible to feel down.

'Exercise and healthy living give you so much! They provide you with a real sense of self-confidence, inner strength, and feelings of empowerment. It's true that you can have all the money in the world, but if you don't have your health, you have nothing.'

Shannan Ponton: Master Trainer and Strength and Conditioning Coach

Shannan Ponton has lived and breathed sport ever since he was a kid. 'My mum and dad were really fit and have always been a huge inspiration to me,' he enthuses. 'From a very young age I was training regularly and running around the block with Dad. I was in my teens when I started playing rugby professionally and became a strength and conditioning coach by the time I was 20.

'I love being active,' Shannan says. 'For me, exercise is everything: it is my absolute priority because it allows me to function at a much higher level in every other aspect of my life. When I train I'm a lot more focused, sharper, and happier in my soul. I love trying new and different things. I thrive on challenging myself and working towards goals.'

Shannan explains that the benefits of training regularly are much more than just looking great. 'Exercise and competing provide you with a real buzz. It's about proving yourself on a daily basis and keeping the fire burning within. It motivates you to be the best you can be, and to live life to the full.'

Adro Sarnelli, Season I

Before: 136.5 kilograms
After: 85.2 kilograms

Since appearing on Season 1 of *The Biggest Loser* and taking out first place, Adro has become an inspiration to many. After losing over 51 kilos on the program, Adro attributes his success to accepting accountability for his actions and ultimately taking responsibility for his life.

Living by his personal motto of 'Eat smart, move more, think thin', Adro has continued to employ *The Biggest Loser* techniques since leaving the house and has dropped several more kilos.

Growing up in Sydney's west, Adro was always a large kid, whose diet consisted primarily of carbohydrate-heavy pasta, bread and potato dishes. By the age of 12 Adro had already visited a dietician, but his weight continued to balloon as he grew older. Tipping the scales at 155 kilograms shortly after the birth of his daughter, Adro confesses that he was deeply troubled by his weight.

'I was a closed, angry and very uncertain person,' Adro says of his old self. 'I wanted nothing more than to be left alone. I was extremely negative.'

He says his turning point on *The Biggest Loser* came when the cast visited Camp Eden. 'I'd always had a fear of heights,' explains Adro. 'My challenge was to jump from a 65-metre-tall tree with only a light harness attached. I was scared beyond reason and stood there for half an hour deliberating, not knowing if I could do it.

'But as I jumped, I began to chant "The New Me!" and everything in my life up until that point flashed

before me. In that moment I saw the taunting I had endured as a kid and recalled the years of feeling depressed; I knew that I didn't ever want to go back.'

Until then, weight loss had primarily been a 'physical task' for Adro, and his main focus had simply been 'to get out of the kitchen and into the gym'. After taking the life-changing leap, he says, 'absolutely everything in my life began to change for the better'.

Since that day, Adro Sarnelli has incorporated his 'New Me' philosophy into every aspect of his life. He has now left behind his old job in the car industry and started up his own successful business, inspired by his new-found mantra.

'I owe everything to *The Biggest Loser*,' says Adro. 'I finally learnt the difference between merely being alive and really living life. Australia is currently experiencing an obesity epidemic and I want to inspire and encourage other people to believe that losing weight and starting a new life is possible. If you are willing to believe in yourself and put in the hard work, it can be done!'

Tracy Moores, Season I

Before: 109 kilograms
After: 87 kilograms

Tracy Moores was one of Australia's original 'plus-size' models, making a living from being a size 16–18. She was beautiful, in demand and loved her work. The only problem was that she used her career as an excuse to avoid living her best life.

'I had always been a big girl but after having three children – one in my twenties, one in my thirties and then one in my forties – everything began to sag. I used the excuse of being a larger sized model to hide the fact I was unhappy about the way I looked.'

As her weight increased, Tracy became more and more inactive. 'I played A-grade basketball,' she says, 'but in the end my weight prevented me from moving forward. As the years passed I knew deep down something had to be done.'

For Tracy, food served as 'a form of entertainment' and she would resort to eating large quantities when she was bored. 'I also overate when I was stressed. I work in the fashion industry, which means enduring long hours where it's tempting to fuel up on carbs.

'I had heard about *The Biggest Loser* but because we were in the first series, I had never seen the show. I went into the house thinking it was going to be a bit like a Camp Eden–style holiday – was I in for a surprise!'

As the weight slipped away it became easier for Tracy to be more active. 'When I left the house I began working part-time

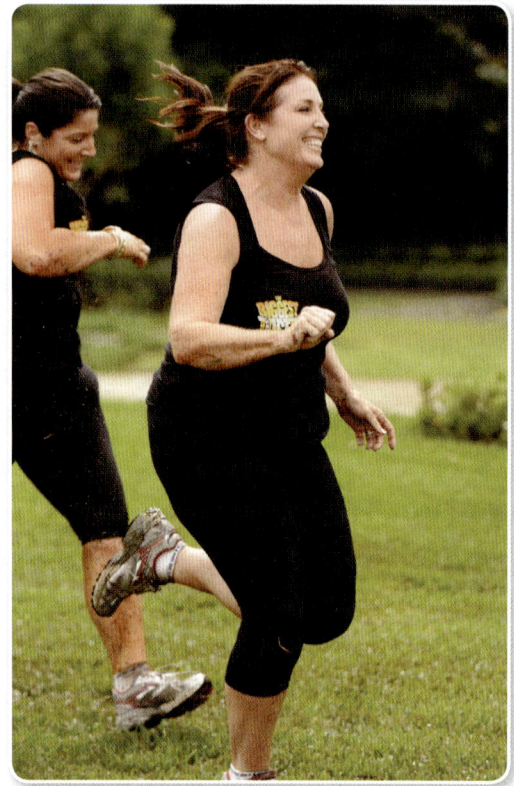

at a gym which allows me free access to the facilities. This is wonderful, as training and keeping fit are now a regular part of my life.'

Tracy also learnt to eat small meals regularly, and how to resist the temptation to binge on sugary food when she is tired. 'I have realised that weight loss is really a battle of the mind. If I am on the verge of reaching for a "treat", I stop myself now and ask, "Why am I doing this?" If it's for emotional reasons, I do something else, like going for a walk.

'One of the most important lessons I learnt on the show was the value of putting myself first. As women, wives and mothers we are so used to putting our husband's and children's needs ahead of our own. Now I ensure I take time out for myself to relax and train, and I am a better person as a result. I am happier than I have ever been!'

Munnalita Kyrimis, Season 2

Before: 127 kilograms
After: 74 kilograms

Munnalita, the owner of a hairdressing and beauty salon, had always been big. As she grew older she learnt to disguise her weight by choosing her clothes carefully and spending hours on her appearance before leaving the house. 'I always felt like I was hiding behind my hair, make-up, accessories and false nails,' she admits. 'I felt that if I prettied up my nails and clothes and put on more jewellery then people wouldn't notice my weight. No-one knew how hard it was, keeping up with all the effort. More than anything I just wanted to be "normal".'

A self-professed emotional eater, Munnalita used food as way to deal with unwanted feelings and crisis situations, until one day she tipped the scales at 127 kilograms. At that point it was a struggle just to make it to the letterbox and she knew she had to make a change for the better.

Munnalita says her time on *The Biggest Loser* allowed her to push through her fear barriers and do something she had never done before – train hard. 'The show gave me a new sense of willpower,' she says, laughing. 'I was always the worst kid at sports day and suddenly I was turning things up a notch, working out at the gym and running up flights of stairs.'

The effort paid off and after shedding a whopping 55 kilograms Munnalita relishes a new-found sense of freedom. 'I have so much more energy now. When I wake up I feel excited. I don't have to spend two hours getting ready and I no longer worry if I don't feel like doing my hair and make-up. I can just put on a summer dress and a pair of thongs and walk out the door.'

Pati Singe, Season 2

Before: 120 kilograms
After: 72 kilograms

Describing herself as an outdoors person, Pati loves embarking on camping getaways, hiking adventures and trips to the beach. 'I've always loved being outside and just getting away from it all,' she says. 'My local area has some beautiful scenery, but there were so many things that I was unable to do previously because of my weight.'

'Being overweight was terrible,' Pati continues. 'Even though I have an adventurous spirit I was leading a very limited life. I lacked the confidence to mix with people and would shy away from social events like barbecues and parties. I went to work, then came home, and repeated this day in and day out. I was completely closed off from the world.'

Pati had always had a large build and says concerns with her weight were exacerbated by her parents' divorce. 'I had a pretty rough childhood,' she admits. 'When my mum and dad split up it affected my confidence and I became very isolated. I didn't let people in after that and just wanted to be left alone. Looking back, my eating was a defence mechanism: it kept me away from the world and prevented me from establishing close relationships and being hurt again.'

Of course the excess weight also stopped Pati from doing things she loved and made enjoying the outdoors almost impossible. 'I had always wanted to go whitewater rafting but my weight stopped me. There was so much I wanted to do but couldn't.'

All this changed when Pati joined a colleague from work and filled out *The Biggest Loser* online application form. A few months later she was in the house, challenging herself mind, body and soul. 'When you start pushing yourself physically, the results are unbelievable! You are doing things you never thought possible and it gives you so much strength on every other level. You gain confidence and this flows into other areas of your life.'

Pati hasn't looked back. Now a healthy 72 kilograms, she says she is leading the life she always wanted. 'It requires work but my quality of life is so much better than before. I am braver both physically and emotionally and prepared to put myself on the line more. It's true that as you lose weight you gain confidence and attract great things into your life, but you are also able to run with opportunities.'

Courtney Jackson, Season 2

Before: 139.2 kilograms
After: 98.3 kilograms

At school Courtney Jackson was always the big kid, and endured relentless taunting and ridicule throughout his teens. 'I didn't have many friends,' he divulges. 'I was constantly the brunt of jokes and felt very insecure. I believed that I wasn't as good as the other kids and felt too self-conscious to venture out to shopping centres, concerts or social events. I didn't attend any formals or proms because I knew I wouldn't be able to get a date. I believed I would never find love.'

As he grew into adulthood, Courtney's weight escalated to the point where his embarrassment 'turned to self-loathing'.

'I gave up all hope and accepted that I would be a fat person forever.' Courtney concedes it was a 'very lonely existence' and that he suffered profound feelings of worthlessness. 'I would look in the mirror and call myself names because I felt so bad about myself and the way I looked. There was a lot of anger there because I hated being that way.'

Courtney worked through his emotional issues in *The Biggest Loser* house but admits it was a tremendous challenge to confront and change his existing thought patterns.

'In the beginning I was incredibly down on myself,' he says. 'I was so used to being negative that it took a lot of time, patience and practice to turn my thoughts

around. My anger had become my defence mechanism, so I was not only working on accepting myself, I also had to find the courage to make new friendships and believe that I deserved it.'

Now 41 kilograms lighter, Courtney feels he has been awarded a second chance at life. Since leaving the show he says he is like 'a phoenix risen from the ashes. I am completely reborn and every aspect of my life has changed.' Not only does he now boast a lean, fit and healthy body, but he has also found direction and a career he loves.

As a personal trainer, Courtney now spends his time helping others lead fit and healthy lives. 'The biggest lesson I have learnt is that I'm worth it,' he adds triumphantly. 'I will never give up on myself again.'

Kirsten Binnie, Season 3

Before: 126 kilograms
After: 71.9 kilograms

Kirsten is a keen sports enthusiast and has represented Australia in water polo. As an elite athlete she was used to putting in the hard yards with her training but after retiring from her sport she gradually gained weight.

Working at a radio station reading the news for the popular morning shift saw Kirsten desk-bound and out of the public eye. 'I woke up at 3 am and worked until midday,' she says. 'Then I would pick up some takeaway on the way home, eat, sit on the couch all afternoon, eat again, then go to bed.' At 136 kilograms, Kirsten slowly became more and more reclusive, holing herself up in her apartment, lacking the confidence to go out. 'You get into a cycle of feeling depressed because of your weight, overeating to cope, and then becoming more depressed. It's living a nightmare you can't escape. During that period I wasted so much time, so many opportunities and a lot of money. It was a sad and lonely existence.'

Luckily for Kirsten, several months in *The Biggest Loser* house saw her shed an incredible 55 kilograms – a result she attributes to staying determined, working out regularly and following a kilojoule-controlled diet. As well as enjoying many positive physical changes, such as feeling more energetic and sleeping better, the one-time elite athlete says she even started to feel taller.

'When you are overweight you try and hide,' she explains. 'You crouch down and you slump your shoulders because you don't want to stand out. As soon as I started losing weight I became aware that I was holding myself differently, with my shoulders back. Now I have a completely different posture. I stand taller than I did before – a result of feeling proud about the way I look.'

Kirsten says shifting the weight allowed her to regain her confidence and take the plunge to move states and begin a new career. 'In the past such a huge change would have really fazed me,' she admits. 'Of course there are still times when it's hard, but overall I feel quite confident that I can handle anything now.'

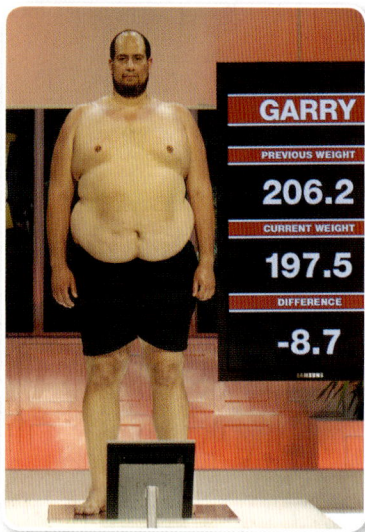

Garry Guerreiro, Season 3

Before: 206.2 kilograms
After: 135 kilograms

At 6 foot 10, Garry is a big teddy bear of a man. Loved by all, he is a happy-go-lucky, friendly character, but his optimistic outlook faded after suffering a broken heart.

'I tried to shy away from the pain,' he says. 'I would go to work, come home, eat something, lie in bed and watch TV – that was pretty much my life.' These periods of isolation were interspersed with frenetic bouts of social activity in an attempt to numb the pain. 'When I wasn't at home I tried to keep as occupied as possible and was going out on self-destructive benders, eating, drinking and smoking all night.'

Garry admits the situation spiralled out of control. Before long he was snacking constantly, raiding the fridge at midnight and indulging in two or three dinners at a time. The one-time active sportsman ballooned from a lean 110 kilograms to over 200 kilograms, which prevented him from playing his beloved basketball and regular indoor soccer and touch footy games. 'As the weight piles on you become prone to injuries, you lose your fitness and feel fatigued. I lacked the energy to do even simple things like walk up stairs.'

When Garry's mood hit rock bottom, he knew something had to be done. With the help of a close friend he applied for a position on *The Biggest Loser* and was successful.

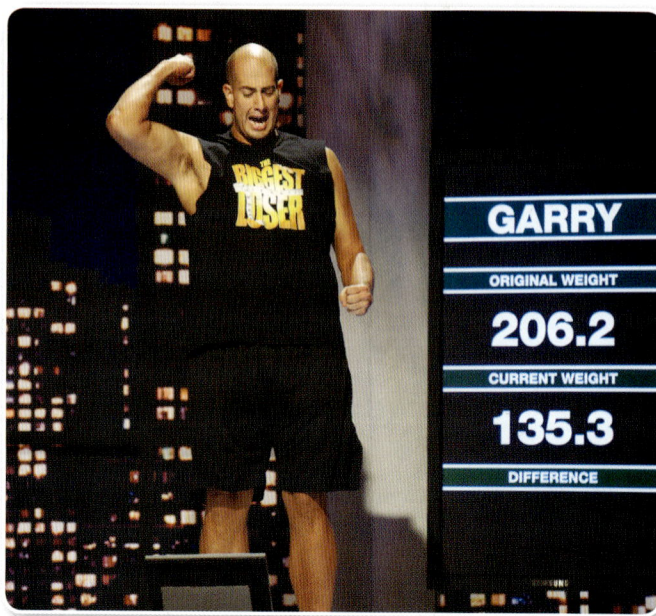

'As the weight slipped away I really started to notice a difference,' he says, smiling. 'You feel more mobile and light on your toes. I felt great physically and started to improve mentally and emotionally as well. One of the best things I started doing in the house was talking about how I felt.'

With the support of the trainers and his room-mate, Garry would vent his emotions rather than trying to 'hold it in' or suppress his feelings by squashing them down with food.

Now Garry weighs a healthy 135 kilos and he has successfully kept on track since leaving the house. 'These days I am a lot more honest with myself,' he declares. 'I used to make excuses for myself about my size or why I couldn't make it to the gym. The truth is you have to be accountable. You need to prioritise and put your health first.'

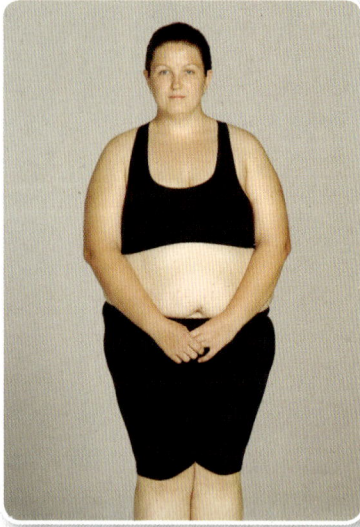

Carrianne Rees, Season 3

Before: 111 kilograms
After: 81.2 kilograms

Carrianne was 24 years old when she joined *The Biggest Loser*. Working as a registered nurse, she found it physically challenging to keep up with the demands of a busy surgical ward. A keen taekwondo enthusiast, she also felt embarrassed when she wasn't able to perform the kicks and manoeuvres like everyone else in her martial arts group. 'My weight was holding me back,' she says. 'I wasn't being the best person I could be and it was depressing.'

To the outside world Carrianne appeared to be a confident person but it was merely a front. 'Before going on *The Biggest Loser* I was absolutely miserable,' she reveals. 'I focused all my energy on my work life because on the inside I was suffering.'

Carrianne sought comfort in food. 'For as long as I can remember I have used food to deal with my emotions,' she confesses. 'If I was happy I would celebrate by eating something decadent with a couple of drinks. If I was depressed I would devour a block of chocolate, which only made the problem worse. Everything seemed to revolve around food. My eating was indicative of my mental state. I repressed my feelings and allowed others to dictate what I should do in my life. I felt like I had lost sight of the real me and relinquished all sense of control.'

CARRIANNE

ORIGINAL WEIGHT

111.0

CURRENT WEIGHT

81.2

DIFFERENCE

-29.8

In the *Biggest Loser* house, Carrianne established a greater degree of authority in her life, and gradually started to turn things around. 'Initially I thought I was going to die, I felt so tired and short of breath from all the exercise we did. But as time went on I became a lot more energetic and enthusiastic about it all.'

Before going on the show, Carrianne's cholesterol and blood pressure were seriously high. 'It was a dangerous condition for someone so young,' she admits, 'but by the end my blood pressure and cholesterol were completely normal. The weight loss restored everything to their perfect levels.'

Carrianne says that one of the best things about being in the house was the fact she could finally distinguish herself from her identical twin sister. 'Up until that point I had always been known as one of the twins,' she explains, 'but suddenly I had my own identity and everybody knew me for me. I was given the opportunity for my personality to shine through and to become a more independent person.'

Since appearing on *The Biggest Loser*, Carrianne has a new lease of life both physically and socially. 'This is the happiest and most confident I have ever felt,' she enthuses. 'For the first time in my life I actually like myself. I have everything to live for.'

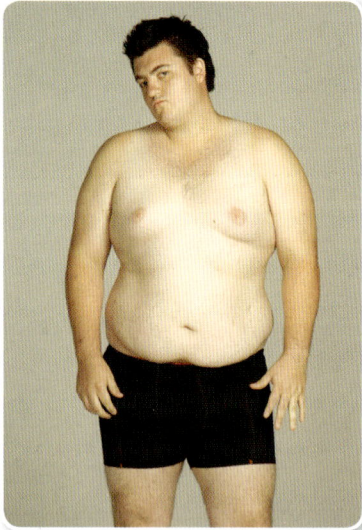

Bryce Harvey, Season 3

Before: 139.2 kilograms
After: 87 kilograms

Bryce is the quintessential young Australian male – he loves his sport, has a great group of mates and relishes life. But although he played sport from a young age he admits he 'always bordered on the heavy side'. At nineteen, he began working two jobs on top of studying for a university degree, and started putting on weight. 'Exercise and sport were put on the backburner, because my main priority was juggling study and work.'

Over the ensuing years, Bryce gained rapidly and steadily, a situation which worsened when he began working in an office. 'I led a very sedentary existence,' he confesses. 'I worked long hours and made poor food choices. I'd grab a quick fix for lunch, visit the vending machine at work, order in for pizza and go to fast-food restaurants. I always took the easiest option, even though I knew it wasn't the best thing for me health-wise. Before long I tipped the scales at well over 100 kilograms.'

Bryce admits carrying the extra weight was depressing and prevented him from enjoying the things he loved. 'I live in Queensland, so a lot of social activity revolves around swimming and going to the beach. I would always be getting offers to join my mates but I made excuses because I felt so self-conscious about the way I looked. I had a real problem with self-esteem and coped by putting on a front. People thought I was happy, but it was all bluff.'

Crunch time came when Bryce discovered he was unable to participate in one of his favourite pastimes: 'I love riding my motorcycle and I was looking for a full set of race leathers but I couldn't find anything that would fit me. It was at that moment I realised how much I was holding myself back.'

After applying online and securing a place on *The Biggest Loser*, Bryce now enjoys an active lifestyle and plays sport regularly again. He has lost 52 kilograms and says he is now more confident than ever.

'Life is fantastic and so different than it used to be,' declares Bryce. 'Before I went into the house I was limiting myself in so many ways, but as I lost weight I literally felt the baggage slip away. I now feel happy to go anywhere.'

Alison Braun, Season 3

Before: 121.7 kilograms
After: 66.5 kilograms

Alison, a loving wife and devoted mother of three children, went onto *The Biggest Loser* with the notion of 'merely losing some excess weight'. What she didn't bargain for was gaining an entirely new life. Describing her old life as 'a prison', Alison now enjoys vibrant health, a new job, an array of hobbies and is living the life of her dreams.

'Before I went into the house I was defined only as a wife and a mother,' Alison admits. 'My whole life centred around that role. I had no interests, no hobbies and there was nothing in my life that was just for me.'

Alison says the weight slowly crept on over the years and as she grew bigger, her zest for life began to decline. 'I started to pull myself further and further away from life and stopped participating in social activities. It happened gradually so I wasn't even aware of it at first. I'd go to the beach with my kids but I was too self-conscious to wear a swimsuit so would stay on the sand, and then I stopped taking them altogether. I wouldn't take my kids bike-riding either, because I lacked the fitness and felt embarrassed about the way I looked. I continually made excuses for myself and just sat on the sidelines watching life go by.'

At 121 kilograms Alison felt like she was trapped: 'I was just existing. From the outside I had it all – a loving husband, three healthy children, a lovely big clean home, a nice car – but the reality is I was totally lost. For my entire adult life I had been a mother and I had no idea of who I really was.'

Over the following months in *The Biggest Loser* household, not only did Alison drop a staggering 55 kilograms, she also launched herself into life with gusto. 'Suddenly I was accomplishing all these incredible feats – like pulling buses, something I had never imagined myself doing,' she states emphatically. 'I was completely and utterly out of my comfort zone yet felt physically and mentally strong for the first time in my entire life.'

Alison says this new-found confidence enabled her to leave the familiarity of her old life behind, ditch her unrewarding job and embrace her future as a keen sports enthusiast, motivational speaker and sales team leader at a gym.

'Every aspect of my life has now changed,' declares the bubbly 35-year-old. 'In my old life I felt hopeless about the future and had absolutely no belief in myself. Now I feel I can do anything I want.'

Amanda Brock, Season 4

Amanda Brock is a talented opera singer with a passion for performing. She's won scholarships and competitions from a young age and has even trained at the Sydney Opera House. 'I love to sing,' Amanda explains. 'When I sing I'm at my happiest; it makes me feel complete.'

But postnatal depression following the birth of her daughter saw her weight soar. 'After I had my baby I put on 55 kilos and it totally eroded my confidence,' she says. 'Opera singing is a very big part of my life, it's the thing I love to do, but after I put on all the weight I lacked the self-esteem to perform publicly. I wanted people to look past my weight and appreciate the beauty of my voice, but in the end the self-doubt took over.'

As well as relinquishing her dreams, Amanda has suffered health problems due to her size. 'I have high blood pressure and cholesterol which are at a critical level, but I'm on medication and am happy to report that both have come down since I've been in *The Biggest Loser* house.'

Amanda is on the show with her husband Stewart, and hopes their new healthy eating and exercise habits will have a positive impact on the entire family. 'We have a beautiful four-and-half-year-old daughter and it breaks my heart that we haven't been able to give her the life she deserves. Stewart and I lack the energy for family activities and as a result our daughter spends too much time in front of the TV.'

'This is crunch time,' Amanda says earnestly. 'I want to lose 55 kilos, start focusing more on my own needs and fulfil my dream to sing. It's an ongoing journey and it won't all be easy, but with drive and determination I have faith I will succeed.'

Starting weight: 170.4 kilograms

Stewart Brock, Season 4

Stewart Brock is an accountant by trade and is regarded by those who know him as a patient, thoughtful and friendly man. 'I'm fairly quiet,' he says, and admits he's comfortable with his opera-singer wife taking the limelight.

'*The Biggest Loser* experience has been great – I'm not one to be the life of the party, so suddenly getting up on national TV is something completely different.'

Diagnosed with a thyroid problem as a teenager, Stewart has since grappled with his weight and says he'd like to learn how to cook healthy meals and stick to a more nutritious eating regimen. 'I'd like to break my old unhealthy habits,' he says. 'My wife (and *Biggest Loser* partner) Amanda and I have become so entrenched in our old lifestyle and eating choices that we need help in making that change. We'd like to really turn things around.'

So far so good. 'Prior to *The Biggest Loser* I was a person who had to retain control. I'm analytical, organised and I have a need for certainty. Being on the show has meant I'm enjoying things I would never usually do. Suddenly I'm out training with the Commando at midnight, being taken off for impromptu excursions, training really hard and pushing myself – physically, mentally and emotionally.

'For the first time ever I realise I don't need to control every situation and am really throwing myself into life.'

Stewart's aim is to lose up to 50 kilos and to reach a good level of fitness so he can lead a more fulfilling and active life. 'After a short time in *The Biggest Loser* house I've noticed a big difference,' he says. 'I lost 13 kilos in the first couple of weeks, which really illustrates what you can achieve when you put your mind to it.'

Starting weight: 136.4 kilograms

Andrew Miles, Season 4

At only 22 years of age Andrew Miles suffered a life-threatening stroke. 'I was feeding my four-week-old baby and had her on my chest when I started to experience some discomfort, became paralysed and couldn't move,' says the self-confessed extrovert. 'That was my wake-up call. I realised that if I didn't take drastic measures my daughter would grow up without a father.

'I was around 150 kilos at that stage, and the hospital told me the stroke was due to being so large. If I didn't change my diet and lifestyle then I was heading for another stroke or heart attack.'

Andrew says he was always an active child, but piled on weight after he stopped surf-lifesaving. The ensuing years were fairly sedentary and overeating was the norm. 'I have a young family to support and in the past my focus has been on work,' he admits.

'When my older brother Nathan suggested we apply for *The Biggest Loser*, I thought it would be a fantastic opportunity to invest all my time, energy and focus into my health. I want to become stronger and fitter so I can support my family, not only financially but also as a present and active husband and father.'

Andrew testifies the biggest transformation since being in the house 'has been psychological . . . Not only am I shedding kilos, my perspective is really starting to change. My dream is to become a police officer and devote my life to protecting the community. For the first time, I know this is a dream I can achieve.'

Starting weight: 144.2 kilograms

Nathan Miles, Season 4

Weighing in at over 145 kilograms, Nathan says his impending wedding is his inspiration to make a change for the better. 'The best present I can give my lovely new wife is a fitter, more energetic and better looking man,' he says earnestly.

Nathan also says he'd like to spend more time being active with his young family. 'Growing up, Mum and Dad would always play sport and games with us, we'd all socialise as a family, and it was great. I regret that I haven't been able to do that with my children because I've always been unhealthy and overweight. I love my kids and I want to give them the best life possible.'

Nathan says his weight became an issue after he suffered a football injury. 'I was playing at state level, then afterwards, when I was no longer training and playing, I was still eating like a footballer. The weight piled on and didn't stop.'

Nathan's goal is to drop seven suit sizes. 'My wedding is a constant reminder of how important this is to me and how much I want to lose weight. Before *The Biggest Loser* I tried on my wedding suit, which was a seven-times extra-large, and that was so disappointing for me. By the time I leave I want to fit into an extra-large; that's my main motivation for being here.

'Wedding photos last forever, they're always on display – I want to feel proud on my special day.'

Starting weight: 145.2 kilograms

Cameron Fisher, Season 4

Cameron is a family man who runs his own business with his daughter and *Biggest Loser* partner Samantha. A self-professed 'foodie', he says his sedentary lifestyle has seen his weight steadily increase to the point where he can no longer do the things he loves. 'I used to race a car years ago. I was a pit manager at Bathurst,' he says, 'but I'm too big for it now.'

Married for 21 years to the woman of his dreams and with three grown-up kids, Cameron is looking forward to an exciting new chapter, 'where my wife and I can spend more time being active and doing things together'.

'The rest of my family are very athletic but I've gradually let my health decline. I'm desk-bound, working 12 hours a day, and am quite relaxed, slow-moving and easygoing by nature. Sammy and I are the two black sheep of the family. It's our hope that *The Biggest Loser* experience will turn things around.'

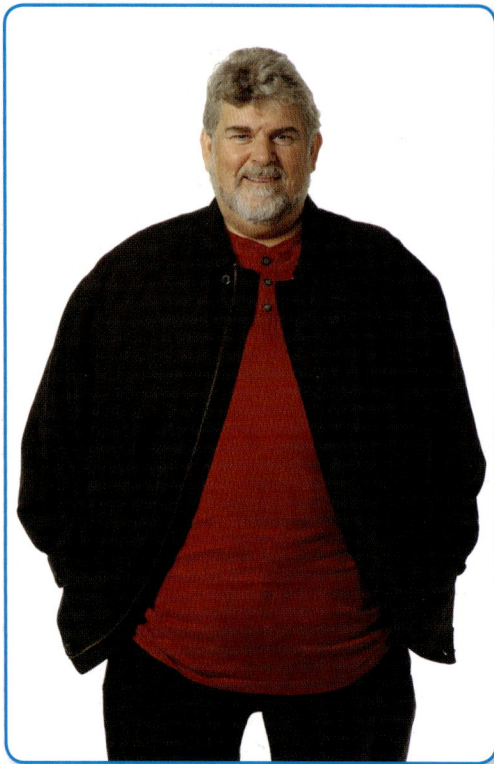

Since being on the show, Cameron has learned to treat his body 'as a business', using *The Biggest Loser* food diary on the internet to keep a tally of his daily calorie intake and the energy burned through exercise. 'When you own a company, you have to do your paperwork. Every month you see how your budget's running and how you're doing, and I've discovered that maintaining your health is just like that . . . Now I just write it all down so I can keep track of things.'

Cameron is seeing results from his hard work. 'I'm looking forward to an enjoyable and active future. When I entered the house I couldn't even run – I used to just sit around and watch TV. Now all of a sudden I'm training each day, and feeling great!'

Starting weight: 164.1 kilograms

Samantha Fisher, Season 4

Sammy is an outgoing woman with a vibrant personality who declares she has everything to live for – a close family, great job and an adoring boyfriend. 'I have an amazing life,' she says, but admits she feels 'held back' by her weight. 'I'm a very happy and confident person, but my weight is the one thing I can't get on top of.'

Sammy's dream of marriage and having kids has been her main motivation for entering *The Biggest Loser* house. 'The doctor has said that if I don't lose weight I won't conceive, and my boyfriend and I would like to get married and start a family quite soon.'

Sammy believes her excess kilograms have prevented her from living to her full potential. 'Being overweight is almost like a disability. There are so many things you can't do – everyday activities that other people take for granted. I can't go to the beach with my friends and I can't go dancing, because I feel self-conscious about being so heavy.'

She admits that shopping trips have ended in tears. 'I can spend all day from 9 am to 4 pm looking for an outfit and still find nothing to wear except for a piece of jewellery, because it's the only thing that fits. Every day my weight brings me down. It takes away from your capacity to enjoy life and be in the moment, because you're constantly worrying about other things – I'm always readjusting my shirt, feeling guilty when I buy food, or thinking of the best way to get out of the car so I don't look too fat. Being overweight plays constantly on your mind and I'd like to get past that.'

The Biggest Loser has allowed Sammy to regain confidence that permanent weight loss is possible. 'I'm determined to reach my goal weight of 60 kilos, embrace life and make the most of every day!'

Starting weight: 118 kilograms

Holly Scouler, Season 4

Holly Scouler, an outdoorsy and active woman, concedes her weight prevents her from enjoying her favourite pastimes. 'I love sports, bodyboarding and motorbike-riding, but it's getting harder and harder and I'd really like to change that,' she says emphatically.

She hasn't always been a big girl. 'Growing up I was quite lean, but then I met my "special someone" and stopped going out and being active. Within a year I went from being a size 8 to a size 18 to 20. It was quite shocking.'

Holly says the turning point came when she saw a photo of herself at an engagement party and realised that her weight had spiralled out of control. 'That's when I knew I needed help,' she confesses. 'I used to be quite pretty, but when you put on that much weight it really alters your looks, not to mention your confidence and self-esteem.'

As well as dealing with her dramatic weight gain, Holly admits she's had to address her attitude towards other overweight people. 'My sister (and *Biggest Loser* partner) has always been a big girl, and in the past I've been quite cruel. I used to give Melanie a really hard time about her size and tormented her throughout our childhood and early teens. But now I'm in the same position and understand exactly how she feels. Not only would I like to lose weight, I'd also love to rekindle the friendship my sister and I shared as little girls.'

Holly also hopes to start a brand-new career working with troubled teens. 'Hopefully my time in the house will allow me to stop doubting my abilities and give me the strength to realise my dreams.'

Starting weight: 108.2 kilos

Melanie Scouler, Season 4

Recently engaged, Melanie says she's looking forward to being a taut and terrific bride. 'I refuse to walk down the aisle the way I am,' she says adamantly. 'I want a beach wedding and I'm determined to change the way I live, so that was my motivation for applying for *The Biggest Loser*.'

Growing up near the beach, Melanie says, made being the biggest girl at school especially hard. 'I've always loved the beachy lifestyle, but I never felt great about myself when I was there. All my bikini-wearing friends were pretty and skinny and I was always the one in the boardshorts. I learned to remain inconspicuous and keep away from the crowds.'

She adds, 'My sister was slim and it made me even more self-conscious about my weight. I'd diet and exercise to try and be like her but it never worked. After a week or so I'd always quit, and then I'd feel like a complete failure.'

Melanie's sister Holly is now her partner in the house. 'We were really drifting apart, but then my sister suddenly put on weight and now we're on the same page. *The Biggest Loser* journey is definitely bringing us closer together,' Melanie smiles.

A naturally outgoing and bubbly person, Melanie says the biggest transformation is taking place within. 'Being on *The Biggest Loser* has been such an amazing experience. My whole outlook is changing. Before I felt embarrassed to go out. I'd try and hide my personality, but now I feel free to be me. There's still a long way to go but for the first time in ages I believe in myself and have faith I can do this!'

Starting weight: 102 kilograms

Meaghan Trattles, Season 4

Meaghan Trattles is a vivacious and fun-loving woman who credits her application for *The Biggest Loser* to a 'moment of revelation'. 'I'd been to a party with all my friends and was having a wonderfully happy time. A few days later we received the photos and it came as such a shock to see how big I looked. At first I thought it was just one bad photo, but then I discovered they were all the same. I was massive. I knew at that point I had to make a decision and there was no turning back.'

It was the trigger Meaghan needed to start reclaiming her health and life. 'Prior to being on the show I'd become extremely reclusive because I felt so bad about myself. Seeing those photos and realising the terrible truth completely robbed me of self-confidence; I lost my zest for living.'

Meaghan confesses she even stopped spending time with family and friends and locked herself away in her room.

'I got to the point where I felt embarrassed if people saw me eating. I used to hide food even if it was healthy, as I felt so guilty and ashamed.'

Thankfully, after taking the leap and appearing on *The Biggest Loser*, Meaghan has a new lease of life. 'I'm a different person now,' she smiles. 'Before the show I knew my future would be dull and dismal, whereas now I'm feeling happy and bright about my path.'

After being single for five years due to feeling 'uncomfortable in my own skin', Meaghan is now hopeful of finding love with a wonderful partner, 'someone I can share my life with'.

'I couldn't have done this without the support and companionship of my mum and *Biggest Loser* partner (Julie). Admittedly, she needed some pushing, but we both agree it's the best thing that's ever happened to us.'

Starting weight: 109.6 kilograms

Julie Trattles, Season 4

As a wife, mum and grandmother, 52-year-old Julie Trattles never imagined she'd be able to train with people half her age.

'I've never felt so energetic or lively!' she exclaims. 'I'm loving being in *The Biggest Loser* house because it's all about me – *my* diet, *my* nutrition, *my* exercise and health! I'm so used to focusing on other people's needs and attending to the family that it feels amazing to finally put myself first.'

Julie reveals that she was slim when she married but gained weight after her three pregnancies. 'I'd try diet after diet,' she says. 'It completely erodes your confidence each time you fail.'

Julie, who is in *The Biggest Loser* house with her youngest daughter Meaghan, lists her aims as 'to be around for as long as possible for the grandchildren' and to 'look in the mirror and be proud of what I see'.

'I'm typically an anxious person and I was really worried I was going to let the side down, but as the days go on I'm getting more and more confident. To be able to keep up with the rest of the people in the house is amazing!' she says gleefully.

After just a few weeks on the show, Julie says the changes have been enormous: she's gone from 'experiencing trouble doing simple things like bending down and picking something off the floor, to working out for an hour or more'.

'I want to feel good about myself,' Julie continues, 'and I also want my family to feel proud of me. I'm suddenly realising that everyone around you benefits when you put your own needs first. After 32 years of marriage, three children and several grandkids, I feel stronger than I've ever been!'

Starting weight: 123.4 kilograms

Ben Terry, Season 4

'There are no excuses now,' Ben Terry declares. An avid sportsman, Ben explains, 'Being big has always been a burden. It's held me back from shining and being all that I can be. I play cricket and baseball at a pretty high level and represent our town at country championships, but when it came to making the New South Wales country side I'd always miss out. I had the ability but they wouldn't pick me because of my weight.'

The 153-kilogram giant is determined to shed kilos through educating himself about nutrition and adhering to a strict kilojoule-controlled diet. 'My knowledge of nutrition is growing every day,' he enthuses. 'I'm learning how important it is to consume protein at every meal and to reduce carbohydrates and sugars.'

Ben is also becoming increasingly self-motivated in his training sessions. 'Before *The Biggest Loser* I continually made excuses about why I shouldn't be active, but now I find any reason to move! I've got aches and pains but I'm not focusing on that aspect at all – from here on in it's all about achieving my goals!'

Ben, who is partnering up with baseball buddy and long-time mate Sean, says he can't wait to be able to buy a 'normal man's shirt'. 'Buying nice clothes when you're this size is really difficult,' he says despondently. 'All the shirts look like huge chequered tablecloths and you end up wearing them all the time because "big men's fashion" is so limited.'

His other desire is to 'be more active with the kids', and he's looking forward to a brand new chapter in his life, with 'increased family time, higher energy levels and greater sporting prowess'.

Starting weight: 153.1 kilograms

Sean Doudle, Season 4

The trigger for Sean to improve his health came when he wanted to donate blood. 'They turned me away because I was too heavy for the beds on the bus,' he says. The humiliation was severe and Sean vowed to get himself back on track.

'I was around 90 kilos when I was 20, but then I suffered an injury playing baseball. I was in plaster for 12 weeks and my weight ballooned significantly.' A 'comfortable and sedentary' home life contributed to further weight gain until he tipped the scales at over 130 kilograms.

Citing bad eating habits as his Achilles heel, Sean is aiming to replace his diet of bakery snacks and takeaway food for more nutritious fare. 'I work as a delivery driver for a baker and I have easy access to hot pies, sausage rolls and cakes. The poor food choices have to stop!'

He's looking forward to being more active when he leaves the house, saying that increased fitness levels will positively impact on his sporting abilities. 'Being overweight prevents you from excelling and being as great as you can be. You can't run as fast as the others and your ability to move is limited. Being this size affects my game immensely. When you're fit and lean you definitely have an edge!'

Sean wants to improve his nutritional knowledge so he can create healthier meals for his family as well. 'I'm the primary cook at home and am responsible for what the kids eat. I don't want them to go down the same path I have, so now's my chance to make some positive decisions and life-altering changes.

'Before *The Biggest Loser* I had a really hard time backing myself. Suddenly I have more confidence and a stronger sense of self. I'm changing mentally and physically and it feels amazing. As the weight comes off, you can feel your spirit lifting.'

Starting weight: 132.5 kilograms

Bob Herdsman, Season 4

At 56 years of age, Bob Herdsman says his time in *The Biggest Loser* house is 'about me doing the best I can'.

'Obviously, I'm competing against people a lot younger and fitter than me and that's a challenge, but ultimately this is my own personal journey and I plan to succeed.'

Bob notes 'obesity is an internal struggle' and the change has to come from within.

'I got to the point where my quality of life was really suffering,' says the grandfather of six. 'I've always loved an active, outdoorsy sort of life, but at my size there's not a lot I can do. My mates and son are keen divers, but I can't go. I can't fit into a wetsuit, and on top of that there are too many risks. If something happened to me, they'd never get me out of the water.'

Bob puts his large stature down to poor dietary choices, excessive portions and slipping into bad habits. The owner of a roadhouse restaurant, he admits to being the 'chief chip tester', taste-testing every batch in the name of quality control.

'My work became an occupational health hazard,' Bob says. 'I was "approving" all sorts of things – hamburgers, chips, pies and sausage rolls. I was already overweight, but when I started the business it just got worse.

'I want to lose weight, I want to be fit and healthy. I have a beautiful wife; we've been together for 40 years and are the best of friends. I have a great family; we all enjoy each other's company and love doing things together. The future holds so much happiness and I'm determined to be around for it. I'm finally on the right path.

'There is no try. Only do.'

Starting weight: 167.8 kilograms

Tiffany Herdsman, Season 4

Tiffany Herdsman admits that almost doubling her body weight in 7 years was physically, mentally and socially debilitating.

'I was 60 kilos when I married my husband and looked and felt fantastic. But then he went to East Timor and I would stay up late at night, reading my book and comfort eating. In the space of a few months I stacked on 8 kilos, and unfortunately it didn't stop. Bad habits soon took hold and then I fell pregnant with my first child and things spiralled out of control. I was bingeing on chocolate and not really caring what I put into my body.'

Tiffany is a self-professed 'family girl' who would love to have more children. 'It's been confronting accepting that I can't have a baby because I'm morbidly obese,' she says sadly. 'I need to learn how to control my eating so I don't jeopardise my health or the baby's.'

Tiffany confesses to feeling a deep sense of shame about being overweight. 'I'm naturally a friendly person, but I let the weight hide who I am. I no longer went to the main street of town because I felt so self-conscious about my size. Being overweight was ruining my life.

'My main goal is to get back to my old 60-kilo self and learn techniques that will keep me slim and healthy out in the real world.'

Tiffany, who has partnered up with her father-in-law Bob, says she's already learned some valuable lessons in *The Biggest Loser* house. 'We've been told that 70 per cent of weight loss is directly due to what we put in our mouths. So Bob and I are being strict about controlling the portion sizes and calorie content of our meals.

'I hope that when I leave the house I'll be a more beautiful wife and active mother. Getting back to a healthy weight will give my hubby and I the best chance of extending our family.'

Starting weight: 113.6 kilograms

Sharif Deen, Season 4

Weighing in at almost 180 kilos, Sharif Deen admits, 'I've always started things and never finished them. I'm determined this time will be different.

'I've been overweight for as long as I can remember and have always promised myself I would get my weight under control. I'd think, "I'll have it sorted by the time I'm 30", but then my 30th birthday came and went. The next goal was to slim down for my wedding – unfortunately I remained big.'

Sharif explains that he grew up in an environment where he was constantly surrounded by food. 'I developed bad habits early in life, because my family showed their love through food. I was a compulsive eater from a very young age: I would eat unconsciously. I was never aware of the calories I was putting into my mouth.'

'My wife is only 55 kilos,' Sharif adds. 'She's very active and I'd like to be able to keep up with her when we go for walks. We'd also like to start a family, but I don't want to bring kids into this world and not be around to see them grow up.'

It was his wife who encouraged him to appear on the show. 'My wife sees the man inside and my size has never been an issue for her. [But] I'd like to change for her so we can have the life we deserve and she can have a physically attractive husband.'

After spending a week with the Commando, Sharif is well on the way to success. Confessing he felt 'close to breaking point', he says he has already noticed significant changes taking place.

'There was a training session with the Commando where we were exercising nonstop for over an hour. I got to the point where my legs were burning and I knew I couldn't go on. I thought "I can't do it", but the Commando gave us no other option. We had to push on.'

Starting weight: 178.3 kilograms

Teresa Hamilton, Season 4

'*The Biggest Loser* journey is about realising your truth,' Teresa Hamilton declares. 'For as long as I can recall I've tried to fulfil other people's expectations. Now I feel I'm finally being honest and getting back to the real me.

'I'm single and I'm on this journey for myself,' she continues. 'I'd like to rediscover my inner strength and adopt a new way of life that will benefit me.'

Teresa says the turning point came for her when she realised her old habits weren't serving her. 'It was a watershed moment, and everything in my life began to change. I've always been an emotional eater, so I'm learning to give up my attachment to food. I've used food as a coping mechanism to deal with some difficult factors in my life, primarily the core belief that I wasn't good enough.'

Teresa confesses that she's spent much of her life worrying what other people think of her, and says she experienced a life-altering epiphany one day early on in *The Biggest Loser* house.

'I'd been paddling a canoe for two and half hours against the current in the Pacific Ocean. At that moment I realised it's not important how I look or whether I come first, but that I give things my best shot and finish the race. In the past I've always wanted to do well for others, but for the first time ever I didn't care what anyone else thought; I was in the race just for me.'

Teresa, who is in *The Biggest Loser* house with her workmate Sharif, says the prospect of losing weight had previously scared her. 'In the past when I lost weight I also felt like I lost my layers of protection. I felt exposed and pressured to live up to all these expectations of what a woman is supposed to be.'

Starting weight: 115 kilograms

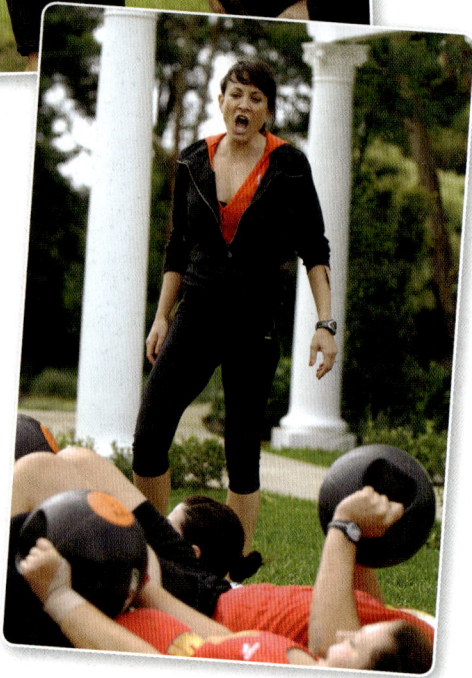

Embrace Your New Destiny

In this book, the Biggest Losers share their winning strategies for:

- Finding the inspiration to get started and revolutionise your life
- Eating right and learning to combat triggers
- Establishing and maintaining an effective exercise regimen
- Handling cravings and temptations
- Learning to live healthily while still participating in everyday life
- Loving the person within and making your health a priority
- Building a support network that will help you remain focused, positive and strong
- Adopting *The Biggest Loser* program in your everyday life to ensure you stay lean, fit and healthy forever!

If you are like most people who have tried to lose weight, you will have realised it can be a challenging journey, both mentally and physically. The Biggest Losers and trainers Shannan and Michelle are here to show you that success is possible and a new body and destiny are within your reach!

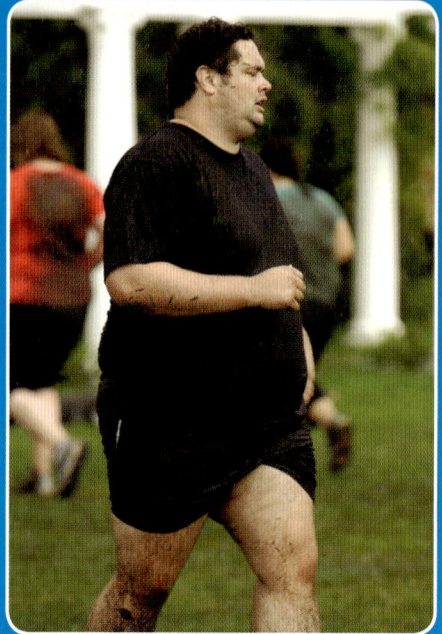

1
A New Beginning

Each of the contestants on *The Biggest Loser* faced a moment when they decided that their current lifestyle and habits were no longer serving them, and realised it was time to make a change.

In some cases it was a health scare that prompted them to take action; in others it was the concern expressed by a family member or friend. It may have been the ongoing emotional battle of being overweight, wanting to be more attractive for their partner, or simply a desire to break free from self-destructive habits and regain a sense of power and control over their lives.

In this chapter you will read about what prompted the Biggest Losers to take that first crucial step. Perhaps their stories will remind you of your own situation and inspire you to take the leap that will transform your life forever.

Munnalita Kyrimis, Season 2: 'I had lost control and knew something had to be done.'

Munnalita was a successful businesswoman, a loving wife, a generous boss and well regarded for her creative talents. In her spare time she built her own houses and did all the interior decorating and landscaping. She was well presented, accomplished and outgoing, and on the surface she appeared to have it all. There was just one problem – her eating was wildly out of control.

An emotional eater since her teens, Munnalita used food as a way to deal with unwanted feelings and negative emotions. As her weight escalated so did her insecurities and feelings of self-doubt. 'I was always conscious of people seeing me and felt terrible being so overweight. I'd walk past shops and see my reflection in the window and then compare myself to the mannequins who were always so thin.'

Munnalita tried to make the best of herself by dressing immaculately, wearing heavy make-up and adorning herself with accessories. But the effort left her weary and she yearned for the day when she could leave the facade behind and 'just slip on a pair of jeans and whack my hair in a ponytail'.

After three years of marriage Munnalita was also incredibly stressed due to several unsuccessful IVF attempts. A much-loved aunt to her sister's three children, she craved a brood of her own. 'The IVF situation and desire to have children put an enormous amount of pressure on my marriage. I was overeating to help me cope, which made me feel even more depressed. Everyone thought I was doing really well but no-one knew what was going on inside and how much of a struggle everything was.'

Munnalita tried many different diets in order to lose weight and aid her chances of conceiving. 'It seemed as though the more I tried to lose weight, the more depressed I felt, and then I overate because nothing was working. I was caught in a vicious circle and knew I had to make a change.'

One afternoon Munnalita was sitting at home on the couch watching TV, feeling upset and agitated. To soothe herself she was 'having a nice little picnic'. She was surrounded by mini lamingtons, a bag of peanut M&M's and other treats when the host for *The Biggest Loser* came onto the screen asking for contestants for the next series.

'It just hit me,' says Munnalita. 'I jumped off the couch and said, "Yes, I'm going to be a Biggest Loser," and had this overwhelming sensation that I was going to be on the show.'

Carrianne Rees, Season 3: 'Food was my way to numb the pain.'

Carrianne was ten when she suffered the agonising loss of her father, and soon after the weight began to pile on. After years of using food as a crutch to help her deal with pain, Carrianne realised that her coping mechanism was actually killing her. Plagued with high blood pressure, cholesterol and fatigue, Carrianne decided it was time for drastic measures.

'I had always been a chubby kid but when my dad died I started to eat for emotional reasons,' says Carrianne. 'Food was always there and it was the thing I turned to whenever I felt lonely or sad.'

Carrianne also stopped playing sports, something she had enjoyed doing with her father. 'I didn't want to play sport any more because it reminded me of Dad. So I stopped being active, hid in my hole away from the world and kept on eating.'

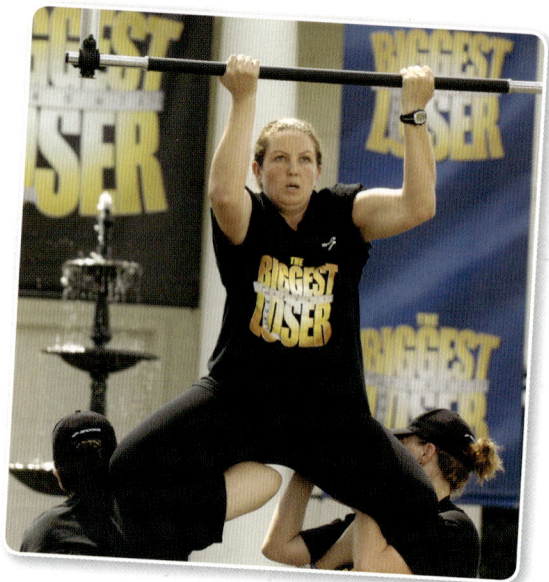

Weighing in at over 100 kilograms, Carrianne knew she was in trouble. As a result she 'tried every diet possible and failed every time'. The problem was that the weight was a symptom of an underlying emotional issue that hadn't been properly resolved. Feelings of loss and heartache were being squashed by an excessive intake of food.

'I knew what I was doing was stupid, that the overeating was destructive and bad for my health, and yet I kept doing it,' Carrianne says sadly. 'Some people numb their pain with drugs and alcohol, others self-harm and for me it was eating. I have no doubt that it would eventually have killed me had I not done anything about it.'

Fortunately *The Biggest Loser* was recruiting participants and so Carrianne went online and submitted her form. 'Appearing on TV scared me because I knew it would be humiliating standing there in my underwear in front of the nation. But I also knew that it was something I had to do. If I went to such great lengths to expose myself and lose the weight then there would be less chance of ever putting it back on.'

Alison Braun, Season 3: 'I had lost faith in myself.'

Alison Braun had been a mother for all of her adult life and focused her energy on 'giving all' to her kids and 'maintaining the perfect household'. But inside she felt empty and wondered if there was a more fulfilling alternative to the life she was leading.

'For fifteen years I merely existed,' laments Alison. 'I wasn't really living and was slowly withdrawing from life.' She lacked the motivation to participate in social occasions, citing her weight as a constant source of embarrassment.

Alison says that she watched *The Biggest Loser* every week and 'absolutely loved it' but was convinced that she lacked the conviction, strength and stamina to appear on the show. 'Every Monday I'd start a new diet and by the evening I would have failed. I had completely lost faith in my ability to take control. I saw myself as a lazy person without a lot of discipline.'

That all changed when Alison happened to see an ad for *The Biggest Loser* and it suddenly dawned that 'perhaps that's how all the other contestants had felt too'. She became adamant that this time would be 'it' and immediately went online and filled out the form.

'I believe it all comes down to making that decision,' she says, 'and deciding how you want your life to be. In the end it is you and only you who can make the change. We all have the keys, it's just a matter of taking the first step and believing you can do it.'

Garry Guerreiro, Season 3: 'I was at rock bottom.'

Weighing in at over 200 kilograms, Garry Guerreiro knew he needed to take action. Spurred on by a close friend, the 6 foot 10 giant found the courage to take the first step and turn his life around.

'I had tried countless diets but the weight kept coming on,' Garry says. 'I was in denial and would just keep buying bigger clothes.' Eventually he knew something had to be done. He confided in a close friend, who became his motivator and an invaluable source of strength. 'She would push me to go to the gym and to eat right because she knew I wasn't happy with my weight.'

When applications were being taken for *The Biggest Loser* it was Garry's friend who took the initiative and made him join. 'Joanne said she wouldn't talk to me unless I applied. She gave me a deadline and made me prove that I had gone ahead with it. A lot of people knew I was in a bad situation but she really went the extra mile. She was prepared to confront me and say, "Something has to be done!"

'You need your friends to be honest with you because a lot of the time you can kid yourself that things aren't that bad. The best thing is for the people around you to have an honest conversation and say, "You need to lose weight, you need to do something about it." If it wasn't for Joanne, I don't know where I would be now.'

Courtney Jackson, Season 2: 'I felt dead inside.'

For Courtney Jackson, the turning point was the most humiliating experience of his life. After lining up for a ride at a popular theme park he discovered he was too large to board.

Up until that fateful trip to the theme park, Courtney had settled for a very limiting life. 'When you are that size you are constantly shunned. I was rejected from jobs because I was too big, as people think you are lazy. The worst bit is you actually begin to believe you are useless so when people react negatively towards you it only affirms what you already think and feel. My life was going nowhere – I felt dead inside.'

Then came the devastating blow: after waiting in line at a theme park for almost an hour, Courtney reached the front only to discover that he was too big for the harness. 'I had to get off and walk past the entire line of about 3000 people,' he remembers. 'I just didn't want to be like that any more. I thought, "Either I change or I will die."'

'I was in the house and still telling myself that I wasn't any good, but after time I learnt to tell myself to shut up. Now I focus on my arms or legs because they are the parts of my body I really like. It's so important to focus on your strengths.'

Courtney says for the first time he now feels in control. 'No matter what happens I know I'll never give up. I never believed that life could be this good; I'll never go back to how I was before.'

Kirsten Binnie, Season 3: 'I felt so embarrassed and humiliated. It was time to turn things around.'

For Kirsten, it was a domestic plane ride that became her trigger for action. Flying from Melbourne to Sydney, she couldn't squeeze into the seat because of her size. After several failed attempts a flight attendant found a man in a larger seat who was happy to swap places.

It was a moment of truth for the one-time elite athlete. 'I remember the look of pity in the gentleman's eyes as he walked past me and sat down in my seat,' recalls Kirsten. 'I sat down and the flight attendant walked up to me just before take-off and offered me an extender belt for my seatbelt. I was already feeling humiliated from having to move seats but to deal with that on top of it just made the situation worse. It was quiet, everyone could see what she was doing and I felt so embarrassed. It was at that point I decided something had to be done.'

Kirsten had been struggling with the most basic tasks, such as doing her shopping at the local supermarket. 'I'd go shopping and by the time I finished I would get back to my car and be all sweaty and red faced. It was horrible and incredibly embarrassing.' Kirsten confided her anguish in her older sister, who promptly encouraged her to go online and apply for the next series of *The Biggest Loser*. This small move so motivated Kirsten that even before entering the household she lost 10 kilograms, a feat she attributes to taking responsibility for her health and making a clear-cut decision to change.

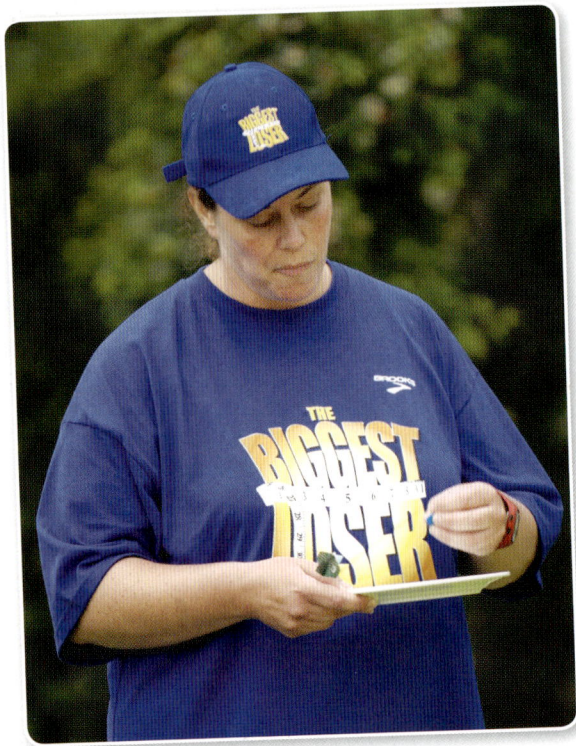

Pati Singe, Season 2: 'I wanted to keep living.'

Pati Singe's defining moment came one afternoon as she prepared to take her dog for a walk. She was sitting down in a chair trying to put her shoes on when she realised she couldn't reach her feet.

'I started to cry,' says Pati. 'I was only 26 years old and I realised that there were so many other things that I wouldn't be able to do because of my weight. I had reached a point where I realised I might not keep living at all.'

This revelation was Pati's tipping point and she has never looked back. 'I knew in my heart that I needed to do something about my situation but it wasn't until a friend at work urged me to fill out a *Biggest Loser* online application that I really made the first move.

'At the time I joined the show I had really isolated myself from the rest of the world. I am a family girl at heart but I shunned the possibility of anyone becoming close romantically. I had basically been living as a recluse and allowed myself to get so big because deep down I thought I didn't deserve the attention.'

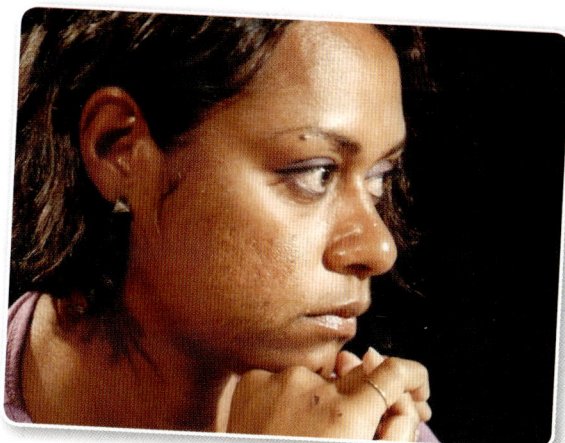

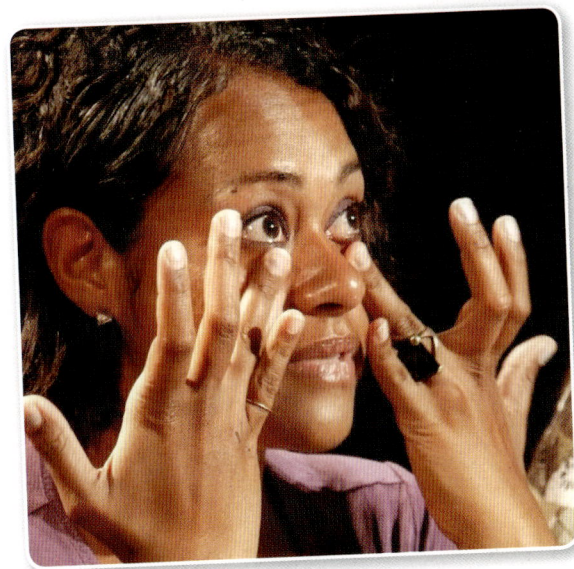

Ready, Set, Go!

If you keep doing the same old thing, you are bound to get the same results. A radical transformation can only occur if you make the crucial decision to do something completely different from what you are doing now. This means having the courage to break with your old routine, embark on an exercise regimen, eat nutritiously and challenge destructive thinking habits.

SHANNAN SAYS

There has to be a pivotal moment in your life where you receive your wake-up call. You don't want to end up in the back of an ambulance saying, 'Gee, I wish I had trained and got my weight under control.' Being overweight is serious. You can die of a heart attack, or lose a leg to diabetes. You feel so bad about yourself you start to hide away in a corner and lock yourself away from life. You don't go out with friends, you don't take your kids to the beach. You have all these dreams and desires just locked away inside you, wanting to be released. It's important to acknowledge you don't have to be this way. You can get your weight under control. You need to cut the excuses and just get into it!

This may seem like a lot of work, but remember that any change in life always requires the greatest energy at the beginning. If you think about a rocket launching into space or a plane becoming airborne, you'll realise that more energy is spent in take-off than at any other stage of the flight. Likewise, the 'lift-off' phase of weight loss always involves enormous effort, but once you start and gain momentum it is guaranteed to become easier.

If you are ready to make a positive change, here are a few pointers from *The Biggest Loser* contestants and trainers to help you on your way.

1 Start with the end in mind

Anyone wanting to achieve great things has to dream the result first. So make a decision to leave your old body behind and then visualise what you want and where you want to go! Remember: whatever you conceive and believe, you can achieve.

Sit down and honestly take stock of your current situation. You need to decide that there is a better life waiting for you. Courtney Jackson, Season 3, says, 'You have to move past the excuses. You only have one body and if you don't look after it, not only will you live a shorter life, you will also live a lower quality of life. You have to make a choice. You have to believe you are worth it.'

2 Set realistic mini-goals

Big goals can seem overwhelming at first. Any major project must be tackled one day and one step at a time. Success is all about the accumulation of small triumphs: Rome wasn't built in a day and it's going to take consistent, concerted effort for you to reach your goal weight.

One of the most helpful things you can do is to break your task up into realistic mini-goals. Set yourself weekly benchmarks, and congratulate yourself when you achieve them. This way you will gain momentum and stay motivated throughout the weight-loss process. Adro Sarnelli, Season 1, agrees: 'Make your goals small and achievable. Instead of aiming to lose 50 kilograms, try losing 1 kilogram 50 times.'

Munnalita Kyrimis, Season 2, also advocates tackling things in small steps. 'The most important thing is just to start,' she says. 'Begin by cutting back. Rather than going out for lunch and having lasagne or schnitzel with chips, have a focaccia. Then the next time have a focaccia minus the cheese. A couple of days after that, instead of the focaccia go for a sandwich with brown bread. There are always excuses why you can't start – something on or some reason why it's not convenient. Don't wait for the ideal time. Just get stuck in. Aim to eat healthily and become active bit by bit.'

3 Keep with the program, no matter what

Courage is not the absence of fear but acting in spite of that fear. As crazy as it sounds, even though you know your old unhealthy habits weren't serving you well, sometimes it's scary leaving them behind. Even though it might feel risky adopting a new way of living, sometimes the biggest risk in life is doing nothing at all. So, despite any challenging or defeatist feelings that arise, stick to your new program no matter what! Tracy Moores, Season 1, says, 'Results are a great motivator. After a while it becomes easier because you can see the rewards for all your hard work. The most important thing is to start and then just keep at it.'

The feeling often follows the action, so if you want to feel great about eating well and exercising, the best idea is to get up and do it!

4 Practise the art of patience

Even though results can take time, they always happen! What you sow is what you reap and the more you put into your weight-loss program, the greater and more impressive your accomplishment will be.

'Patience is really important,' says Garry Guerreiro, Season 3. 'In the past a lack of patience was my biggest hurdle because I didn't really understand the weight-loss process. I wanted to lose all the weight in a week and would become frustrated and give in. When I went on the show my expectations were quite low because I was judging myself on past experiences. But as the weeks went by and I was losing kilos, it began to register that losing weight takes time. It is a game of patience and if you stick to it, you will eventually get results.'

Make the decision to move towards your goal every day and before long you will find you are seeing the results of all your hard work.

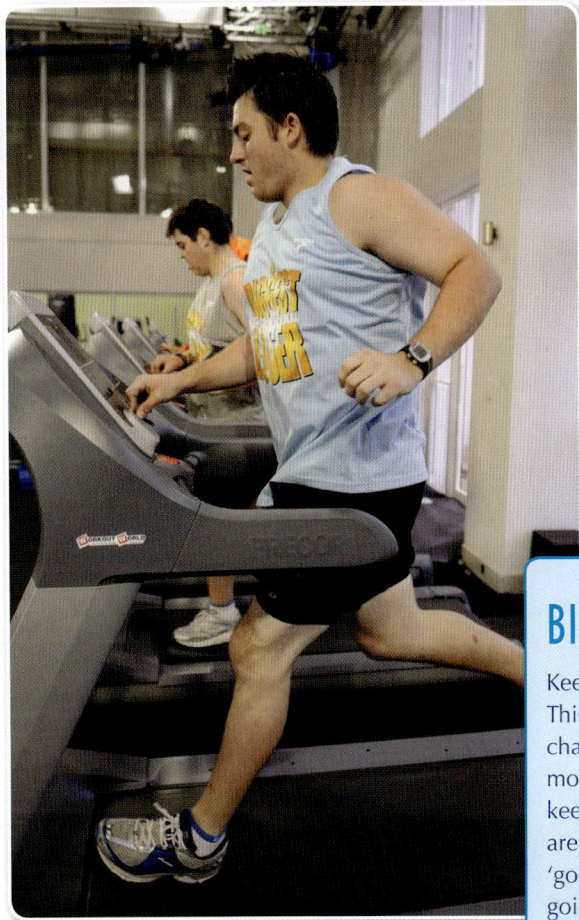

5 Find yourself a cheer squad

It helps to have supportive people around you, and being accountable to someone else can give you a reason to hang in there on the tough days. Whether it be your partner, a friend or coworker, it's good to find someone who can lend some encouragement along the way.

'Recruit as many people as you can,' advises trainer Michelle Bridges. 'You are going to need that support, particularly in the initial stages. Your friends and family should be there to help you as you clean up your diet and get yourself on track.'

Kirsten Binnie, Season 2, agrees. 'It's important to find at least one person who is prepared to help you stay motivated along the way. Better yet, see if you can find someone who will join you on your journey.'

BIGGEST LOSER BIG TIP

Keep in mind you are not just going on a diet. This is a whole new way of life. It takes time to change so you have to be patient. There will be moments when you are tempted to give in but if you keep your eyes on your goal and remember why you are doing it, you will be okay. It's not about being 'good' for a couple of months or even a year then going back to your old ways. It's a gradual process of creating a better, healthier and more fulfilling way of living.

Bryce Harvey, Season 3

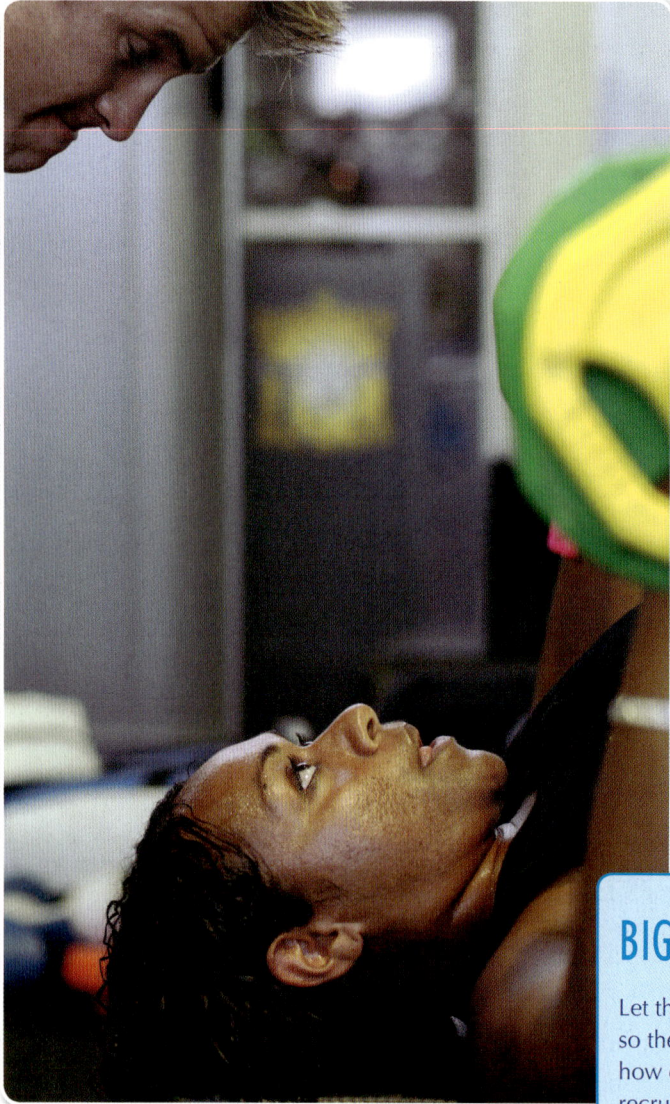

'That way you can adjust your meals together, go walking, and have a friend who understands exactly what you are going through. I am lucky as most of my friends eat really well and take care of themselves. When we socialise we stay away from junk food so it has made things a lot easier after coming off the show.'

Research indicates that having a good support network not only helps you lose weight but makes it more likely you will keep it off. Call a member of your cheer squad whenever you feel challenged and they will remind you how great you are and how far you've come. Recruit them to exercise with you, join in the fun of your new challenge, and invite them to celebrate when you achieve your mini-goals. Remember, people want you to succeed – give them a chance to help support you and be part of your team!

BIGGEST LOSER BIG TIP

Let the people close to you know what you are doing so they can support you. You will be surprised at how eager they are to jump on board. If you can, recruit a buddy to go the distance with you. You will find that you really need that moral support.

Pati Singe, Season 2

6 Be as active as possible

It's a fact that healthy people are physically active, and they incorporate exercise into their lives on a daily basis. Aim for at least 45 minutes to one hour per day. As well as sticking to your regular exercise routine, try to move around more in your daily life. Take the stairs instead of the lift, park your car a couple of blocks away from your destination and walk, do strengthening arm lifts as you carry your groceries home, take an energising walk at lunch with your coworkers – wherever you are, ask yourself how you can incorporate a little more physical activity into what you are doing. Remember, the more you move, the more kilojoules you burn!

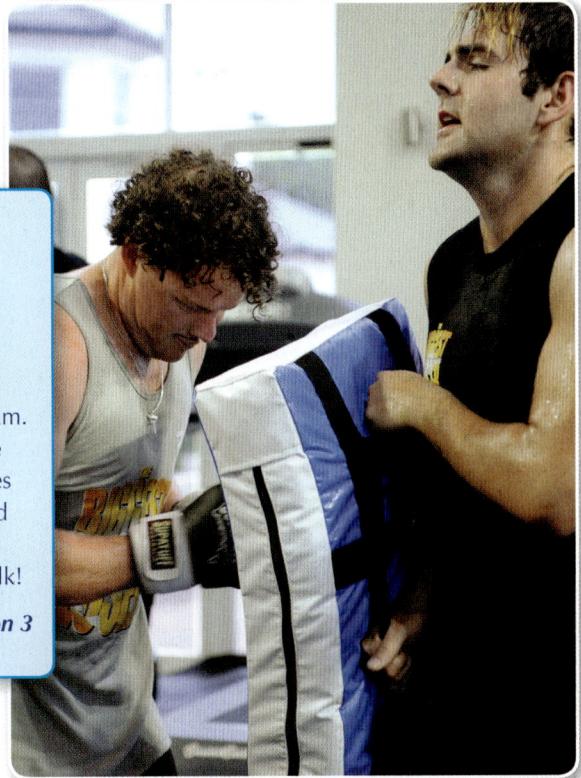

7 Set up a food plan

One of the first and most important things you should do is to set up a daily food plan. Remember that what you put in your shopping trolley often ends up in your mouth, so it's important that you make healthy food choices that fit in with your plan. If it's not on your list, don't let it leave the supermarket!

Adro Sarnelli, Season 1, recommends being prepared. 'Begin by clearing all the junk out of your house,' he advises. 'When you are in a strong state of mind it is important to prepare for when you are not. Creating the right environment for yourself and setting up a plan ensures you will succeed.'

BIGGEST LOSER BIG TIP

When getting started one of the most important things you can do is to have a plan. For breakfast, rather than going to McDonald's and having pancakes, just make it simple. Have one bowl of breakfast cereal with some skinny milk. Enjoy a healthy salad sandwich at lunch and for dinner have some protein like chicken with some vegies. By making healthy changes and sticking to them you will begin to see results.

Munnalita Kyrimis, Season 2

8 Celebrate each day

The happiest people in life are the ones who learn to accept the gifts each day brings. While it's helpful to visualise your final goal, it's just as important to be grateful for where you are now and to relish each stage of the journey. Pati Singe, Season 2, agrees. 'If you don't give yourself a pat on the back once in a while it's easy to lose sight of just how far you've come. It makes a huge difference when you take time out to stop and celebrate each little achievement along the way.'

Learn to appreciate life's simple pleasures such as the sights you see on your daily walk or run, the sense of satisfaction you feel after a workout or the way your clothes feel slightly looser. Treat each step as its own accomplishment and celebrate every day.

As *The Biggest Loser* contestants can verify, the sooner you get started, the sooner you will see results! If you view weight loss as an exciting journey, you should begin as soon as possible in order to arrive at your fabulous new healthful destination. It takes courage to make a change and commitment to see your decision through, but it helps to know that others have stood exactly where you are now and succeeded!

SHANNAN'S **TOP TIPS** FOR GETTING STARTED

1 Find a training partner

It's so much easier with two. You can motivate one another.

2 Set small achievable goals

Don't set out to lose a huge amount straight away. Instead, aim to lose 1 kilogram per week for the first 6 weeks and stick to that.

3 Reward yourself

For every goal you reach, congratulate yourself and give yourself a treat.

4 Clean out the fridge

Throw out all the junk! It might feel wasteful but it will be a whole lot more wasteful putting it inside your body.

5 Get a personal trainer

This is imperative. Starting a fitness regimen without a trainer is like going to the hardware store and buying some timber and nails and saying, 'Right, I'm going to build a house.' You need a qualified builder to guide you and show you what to do. Get a good personal trainer who knows what they are doing and can show you the best way to move forward.

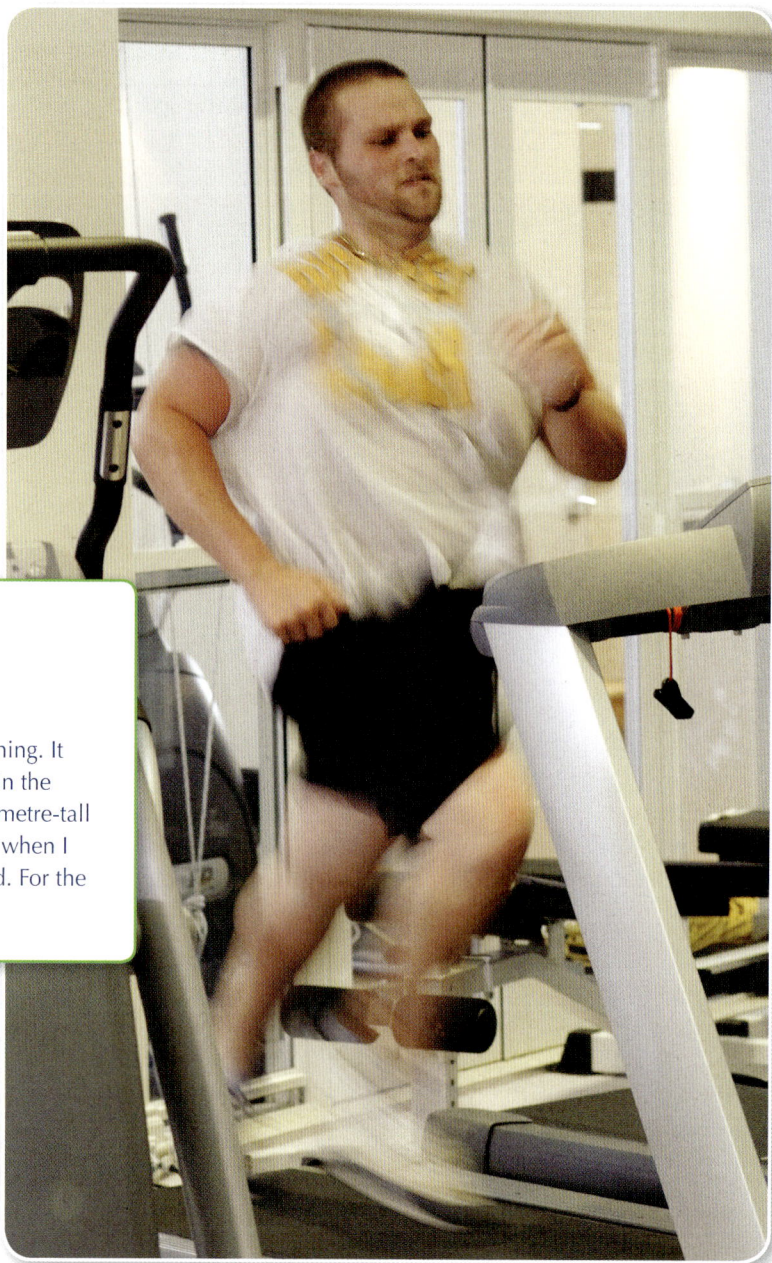

Best Moment:
Adro Sarnelli, Season I

Surprisingly, my best moment wasn't winning. It was attending Camp Eden and partaking in the 'Braveheart jump', where I leapt off a 65-metre-tall tree. That was a defining moment for me, when I knew in my heart everything had changed. For the first time in my life I felt free.

Toughest Moment:
Munnalita Kyrimis, Season 2

My toughest moment came during a temptation. There was a food van outside and we were allowed to go and order whatever we wanted and eat it. I chose a Mars Bar, then decided it wasn't going to be enough. So I asked for another one and ate two whole Mars Bars.

I was training for hours every day, pushing myself to the limit, but when it came to food I was still very weak. I finally had to admit that food had a hold over me and things needed to change.

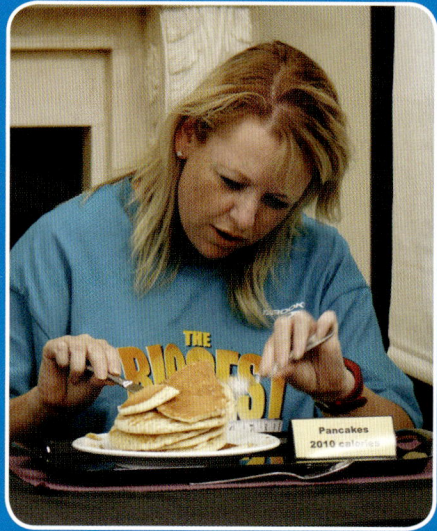

2
Eating Well

As any Biggest Loser will testify, weight loss is not just about the external process of shedding kilos. It is an internal process of learning to view yourself in a positive light, dealing with emotions as they arise and developing reliable coping strategies. In other words, the way you think and feel about food is just as important as following a kilojoule-controlled program.

Eating well always begins with the mind. To start losing weight, you will have to change the way you think about food. In many cases, people who overeat have stopped seeing food as a delicious fuel. Instead they treat it as an emotional anaesthetic to help block negative or unwanted feelings. The good news is that it is possible to turn things around with a few psychological and practical techniques that will change your relationship with food forever.

Choice, not circumstance, determines success, so by mapping out your plan and making some informed food decisions you will be employing a winning formula to achieve your goals.

In this chapter you'll discover the practical strategies – both mental and physical – employed by *The Biggest Loser* contestants as they learnt to adopt new and effective diet and lifestyle habits.

Your body is a reflection of your thoughts so it's important to think about yourself in the most positive light possible. As any professional sportsperson or Olympic athlete will tell you, visualising results is an imperative part of their winning formula. One of the most effective techniques you can employ when losing weight is to take some time each day to visualise how you want to look and feel. Find somewhere quiet, close your eyes and see yourself as lean, healthy and strong.

BIGGEST LOSER BIG TIP

'You have to believe it before you can achieve it.'

I knew that if I focused on becoming fit and healthy, I would lose weight as well. I didn't aim for a particular body shape as such, instead I visualised myself doing things I had enjoyed in the past – getting back in the water and playing water polo, going shopping without breaking into a sweat, and walking up the street without getting all red and puffy. My main aim was to complete activities without becoming breathless or embarrassing myself. I saw myself fit and healthy and going about my daily life like any other normal person.

Kirsten Binnie, Season 3

It doesn't have to take a lot of time. 'Even if you start with just 5 minutes, use that time purely for the sake of thinking positively about yourself and focusing on your dreams,' recommends Carrianne Rees, Season 3.

Imagine yourself as you would like to be in one year, five years and even in ten years. What do you want to look like? What sort of person do you want to be? Do you see a healthy, happy, vitality-filled future for yourself? Imagine yourself at your goal weight and envisage success! It may help to picture yourself at an upcoming celebration in a fabulous outfit – then apply that vision every day to stay on track. If you start to see yourself as the person you want to be, before long your mind will start believing it.

Munnalita Kyrimis, Season 2, says, 'When I was in *The Biggest Loser* house I would train in the gym and visualise myself wearing a size 10 pair of jeans, with my hair in a ponytail and sans make-up. Every day I would see myself how I wanted to be. I would imagine myself on finale night, looking slim and glamorous. This got me through the tough training sessions.'

Remember, you are your possibilities, not your circumstances. You can do anything you dream and are prepared to work for!

Plan Your Meals

On the show, each contestant's food intake is determined by their weight and the amount of exercise they do. Their daily food allowance is then divided between three main meals and two snacks.

As *The Biggest Loser* contestants can vouch, your mind and body have an incredible ability to adapt to change when you tackle things step by step and have a clear guideline to follow.

Knowing what you are going to eat each day is vital to staying on track. It allows you to feel in control and helps you stay organised. If you plan your meals, you know exactly how many kilojoules you are ingesting and how much exercise you need to do that day to keep losing weight.

SHANNAN SAYS

I recommend making food as plain as possible, at least in the initial stages. Plain food makes eating a chore and reduces the desire to consume it. I'd recommend planning three small meals a day and a couple of snacks if required. Healthy snacks include ham with cottage cheese, or some cottage cheese and chopped capsicum wrapped up in lettuce. The best idea is to make sure all your meals are protein based. Also, if you cut your carbs out at night, you'll get a much better result.

Spectacular achievements are always preceded by painstaking preparation, and weight loss is no exception. By knowing exactly what your daily food quota looks like you will be less inclined to go off the rails. Become familiar with the kilojoule content of food so if you do slip up you can make the necessary adjustments. For example, if you decide to have an extra slice of bread at lunch, try to cut down on your carbohydrate intake at dinner by choosing green leafy vegetables, or simply up your exercise regime that day to burn off the extra kilojoules.

BIGGEST LOSER BIG TIP

'Planning is everything.'

My secret is to plan. I recommend buying the Biggest Loser Calorie Counter and reading up on the energy content of everything you eat, as you may be surprised! I eat three main meals a day, including lots of lean meats and fish with plenty of vegies and salads. Before *The Biggest Loser* I would typically grab fried foods but now I will make a healthy dinner – one of my favourites is homemade pizza with mountain bread, chicken and vegetables. It's tasty and low in calories. For snacks I have fruit – like mandarins, strawberries, apples – and even celery. The main thing is to devise a daily food plan, then stick to it!

Courtney Jackson, Season 3

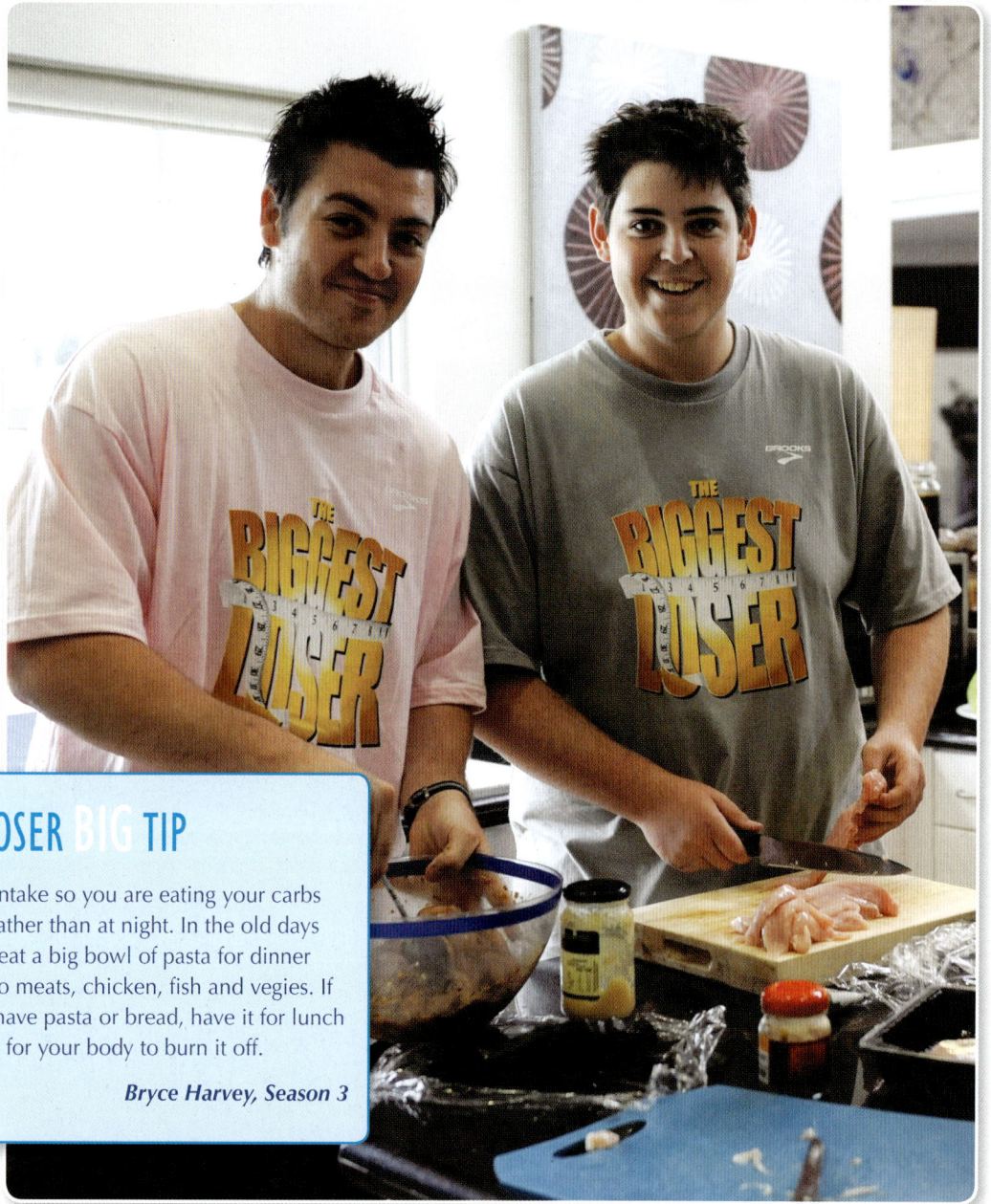

BIGGEST LOSER BIG TIP

Plan your food intake so you are eating your carbs during the day rather than at night. In the old days I would usually eat a big bowl of pasta for dinner but now I stick to meats, chicken, fish and vegies. If you're going to have pasta or bread, have it for lunch so it allows time for your body to burn it off.

Bryce Harvey, Season 3

Make Healthy Choices

One of the first and necessary things to do as you embark on your eating program is to make a clean sweep of all junk food. This means removing 'problem' food from the fridge and pantry and making sure you stock a healthy trolley at the supermarket.

Wherever you are, you should think, act and eat like a fit person. This means eradicating your regular comfort foods and replacing them with healthy, more nutritious options. Nutritionists advise that to lose weight and keep it off, it helps to eat protein at every meal. In fact, in a new study published in the *Journal of Clinical Endocrinology and Metabolism*, researchers discovered that the regular consumption of protein actually helps suppress the release of ghrelin, a hormone secreted by the stomach that stimulates appetite. When balanced with 'good' carbohydrates (such as fruit and vegies) and healthy fats, a diet high in protein is an effective weapon in the fight against flab!

MICHELLE SAYS

Protein is essential for rebuilding muscle and for keeping you feeling satisfied. Great forms of protein include egg whites, cottage cheese, a piece of fish or a small piece of steak. Sometimes it can be hard to get protein into every meal, which is why I often have a protein shake in the morning.

Eating Well Every Day

Food is too important a part of life not to enjoy it. Focus on the delicious goodies you *can* eat, rather than the guilty pleasures you're trying to avoid. Make sure every meal is a taste sensation so you feel nourished and satisfied, not deprived and cranky.

There are any number of good food plans around you could follow, including the excellent example on the Biggest Loser Online Club. Whichever diet you choose, remember there are three golden rules.

1 Don't go without!
You should have three meals and two snacks a day to keep your metabolism firing and to make you more likely to resist temptation when it inevitably arises.

2 Eat loads and loads of fruit and vegetables.
Why? Because they provide huge amounts of natural goodness for very few calories in the form of carbohydrate, fibre and life-enhancing vitamins and anti-oxidants. The old truism 'everything in moderation' does not apply to fruit and veg. Most people regard them as an accompaniment to everything else when, in fact, they should be the main deal. So, bulk up your protein with veg and you won't add bulk to your frame.

3 Eat lots of variety.
Do you eat the same breakfast cereal every single day? Don't get stuck in a food rut but treat your tastebuds by eating widely. Not only will you enhance your pleasure, you will also capture as many different nutrients and protective food chemicals as possible.

A day of healthy eating could go something like this.

Breakfast: Avocado on soy and linseed toast with a good squirt of fresh lime juice or low-GI muesli with berries, mango and banana and a big dollop of naturally sweetened yoghurt.

Lunch: Turkey or roast beef sandwich on rye with a scraping of avocado, lettuce, tomato, cucumber, blanched beans and grated carrot or chunky chickpea salad with roasted vegetables, rocket, cherry tomatoes and a zesty citrus dressing.

Dinner: Chicken or tofu stir-fry with baby corn, snow peas, Chinese greens, red capsicum, chilli and ginger, finished with hoisin sauce and served with soba noodles or grilled fish and a white bean salad with olives, sundried tomato, broad beans, rocket and cucumber.

The Biggest Loser contestants are warned against the 'white foods', including pasta, rice, sugar and flour, which all spike blood sugar levels and induce cravings. You will need to eliminate alcohol, at least for now. Not only does alcohol add extra kilojoules to your diet, but it is also a known depressant and slows everything down – including your metabolism.

The importance of drinking water cannot be overstated, as it is essential for keeping the body functioning properly. The human body is composed of approximately 70 per cent water, and as well as contributing to circulation, transportation of nutrients and digestion, water is also known to keep hunger pangs at bay. Kirsten Binnie, Season 3, says, 'Drinking water is an excellent way to avoid temptations and to keep yourself feeling full. You should be drinking at least a couple of litres a day.'

Remember, The Biggest Loser program isn't a short-term diet – it is a plan for life. This means adopting healthy eating habits and choosing nutritious options everywhere you go – whether it's in the office, out at a restaurant, or at home.

BIGGEST LOSER BIG TIP

It's so easy to resort to the convenience of takeaway. Being healthy takes more effort and requires planning – but it is worth it! Try packing your lunch, or cooking dinners on the weekend, freezing them and eating them during the week. The payback is that you are eating healthier, will have more energy and feel better within yourself.

Tracy Moores, Season 1

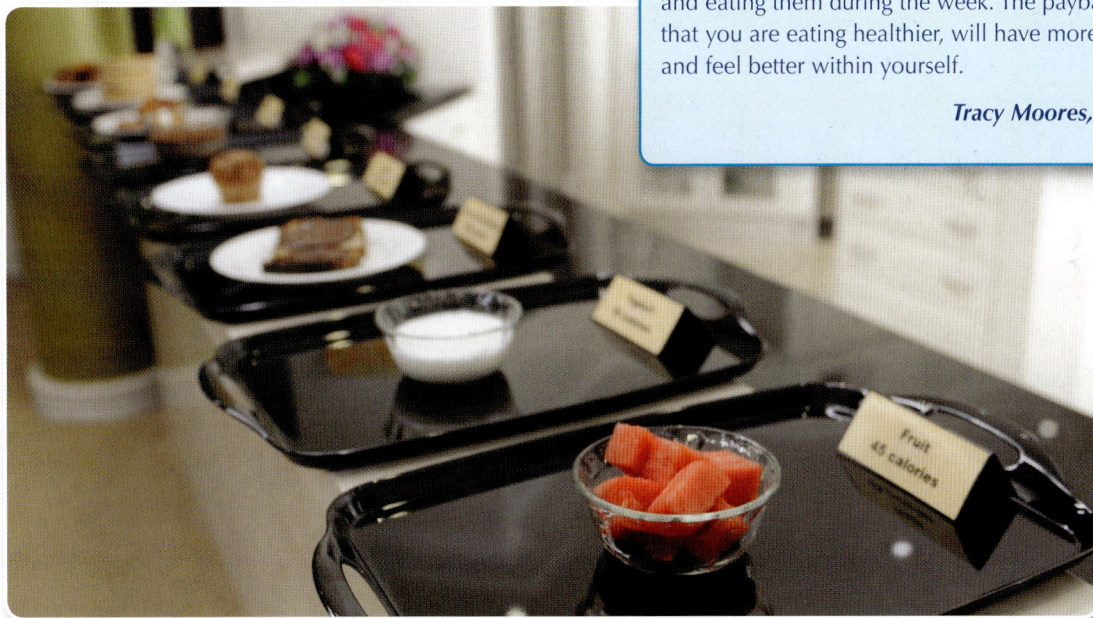

BIGGEST LOSER BIG TIP

'I don't need junk food any more.'

In the past I overate for emotional reasons. I had a broken heart and that's when I started bingeing on unhealthy foods and stopped playing sport. Before going into the *Biggest Loser* house I would always have a hankering for fast food and several times a week I would eat takeaway – a chilli chicken burger with chips. I didn't think twice about it. I was so reckless for so many years and felt totally out of control.

   Since coming out of the house I have had a chicken meal once but that's all. I have a different approach now. Before food was the key to trying to feel better but it always backfired. Now when I am upset I talk to the people close to me, or I go for a walk or to the gym. I watch what I eat and I don't rely on food any more.

Garry Guerreiro, Season 3

Eat Regularly

As soon as you have started visualising a new, healthier you, eliminated junk food from your pantry and fridge, and developed a balanced food plan, the next thing is sticking to it! *The Biggest Loser* diet calls for eating regular meals – a stipulation the contestants must adhere to.

As Michelle notes, *The Biggest Loser* trainers and contestants advocate eating a healthy breakfast – always – because breakfast gives your metabolism a jolt. This is called the thermic effect and it happens each time you eat. Your metabolism slows down when you are asleep and the only way to speed it up to optimal levels again is to eat. So by having a bowl of fibre-rich cereal with low-fat milk, or a slice of toast and an egg, or a bowl of yoghurt and some fruit, you are effectively turning on your fat-burning mechanism for the day.

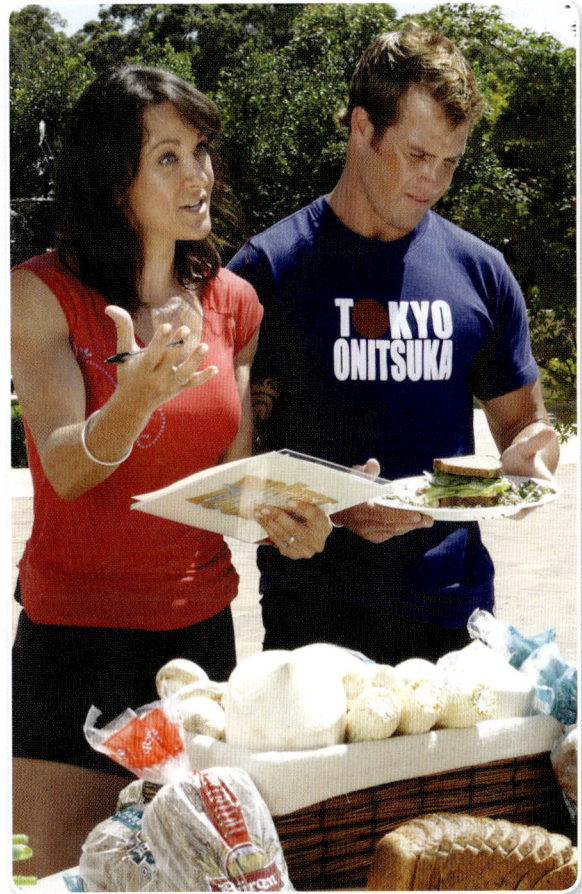

MICHELLE SAYS

Missing meals only plays havoc with your metabolism. It's vital to eat three main meals a day. A lot of people skip meals, only to overcompensate at night. And then because they binge at night, they wake up the next morning and won't be hungry, and so the cycle continues. The body is like a furnace and to keep it running efficiently you need to eat. You actually increase your metabolism slightly when you eat a meal, so by having regular meals it keeps your metabolism up and rolling.

The British Nutrition Foundation says that eating a good breakfast can help people control their weight. This is probably because when people eat a substantial meal first thing in the morning, they are less likely to feel hungry before lunch and snack on foods that are high in sugar and fat. Continuing to eat regularly throughout the day builds on that good start, keeping your metabolism firing and warding off the possibility of binge eating.

According to the Eating Disorders Foundation of Victoria, missing meals in an attempt to lose weight is worse than ineffective: it may actually *promote* weight gain. This is because when your hunger catches up with you it is likely to be more intense, prompting you to consume a larger amount of kilojoules than if you had stuck to your meal plan. Katherine Tallmadge, MA, RD, author of *Diet Simple*, says, 'People go too long without eating, and then pig out when they are ravenously hungry.'

If you stick to your food plan, consuming a portion of protein at each meal, your body receives all the fuel it needs to efficiently burn fat.

Kirsten Binnie, Season 3, has learnt the value of eating breakfast every day. 'You need to have breakfast, you need to have a snack, then lunch, another snack, then dinner,' she says. 'Your body needs small portions of healthy food regularly. For breakfast I have a small bowl of cereal such as oats or muesli with low-fat milk; for lunch I have vegies with rice or pasta, a sandwich, or soup and a crusty roll; and dinner is meat and vegetables. For snacks I enjoy a banana, apple, a handful of cashews, carrot with hummus or low-fat yoghurt.'

SHANNAN SAYS

I suggest an eating plan that is high in protein, low in carbs and definitely low in fat. By sticking to this formula and eating regularly you keep your metabolism up and insulin levels down.

How to Deal with Emotional Eating

One of the major reasons people overeat is due to emotional factors. Compulsive eating or overeating often signify that food is being used to squash down unwanted emotion. Whether they are feelings of boredom, loneliness, emptiness, sadness, anxiety or frustration, food can serve as a powerful release. But the sense of comfort from overeating is short-lived, leading to further negative feelings of guilt and shame.

If you are an emotional eater you should investigate the causes of your eating and the way you feel about yourself and your life. Perhaps you feel unfulfilled in your present job, or eating has become a way of dealing with stress. Maybe you live alone and use food as a way to alleviate boredom. Whatever it is, emotional eating is often an indication that there is something wrong in your life that needs to be addressed.

Some sure-fire signs of emotional eating include:

◗ eating when you are not hungry
◗ eating at night
◗ using food as a source of comfort.

Many of *The Biggest Loser* contestants confirm that night eating was a particular problem. As world-renowned trainer and author Bob Greene explains,

'Night eaters are often eating in response to anxiety or to the emotional turmoil they have experienced throughout the day.' He suggests that the best way to deal with this problem is by establishing a cut-off time for yourself and to abstain from eating for at least two hours before bedtime.

Jill Ball, co-author of *Beating the Blues* and an expert in eating disorders, says another effective way to combat emotional eating is to use the 'delay and distract' technique. Whenever you feel an urge to repress your emotions with food, simply walk away and do something else for 15 minutes. Chances are the emotion will pass and with it the compulsion to eat.

Adro Sarnelli, Season 1, says, 'I am now at the stage where I can stop myself from eating for emotional reasons. I recognise the signs, so I immediately change direction and do something else. Everybody can do it: it's just a matter of time and practice. In the meantime, recruit all the help you can get.'

Some useful distraction activities include:
- phoning a friend
- going for a walk
- heading to the gym
- pampering yourself with a face mask
- doing some gardening
- turning on your favourite music and dancing
- painting your nails
- writing in your journal
- sending an email
- indulging in a luxurious bubble bath
- keeping yourself occupied with a crossword puzzle
- moving – any way you can!

Whatever you decide to do, make sure the activity is enjoyable and will enhance your mood.

Another effective tool used by *The Biggest Loser* contestants and recommended by psychologists is the application of cognitive therapy behaviour techniques (CBT). What we choose to focus on and the thoughts we think have a strong influence on our moods. To feel happier and more in control of your life it is essential to challenge any negative thoughts as they arise. When you feel bad about yourself or a situation, write down what you are thinking. Then challenge this thought on paper – is the thought helpful, is it true? Finally, jot down a more helpful belief or positive way of viewing the situation.

By employing cognitive behaviour techniques you will learn to challenge unhelpful thoughts and beliefs and deal with your emotions. The next time you are down, remember that what you think affects your mood – challenge the thought and the chances are your negative emotional state will vanish.

Food is often used to alleviate feelings of loneliness. According to the Australian Bureau of Statistics, the number of people living alone is on the rise, with as many as one quarter of all Australian households now containing only one person. Social isolation is a concern for many. If this is the case for you and you find yourself yearning for companionship, it is vital to stay in touch with friends and family and participate in hobbies, sports and pursuits that interest and captivate you. Attend your local church, join clubs that focus on your passions, relax in your local park, become a tourist in your own city, get together with friends for social events, volunteer . . . Reach out and become involved in life! By learning to fill the void with things other than food, not only will you boost your emotional state, you will ultimately lead a more fulfilling life.

Keep a Food Diary

One of the most effective and useful ways to aid weight loss is to keep a food diary or journal, recording everything you eat and documenting the day's events so you can pinpoint why you turn to food for comfort. It also allows you to keep track of your exercise and to calculate the kilojoules burned.

Keeping a food diary or journal is a powerful tool for self-discovery. By taking stock of what you eat, when you eat it, where you eat it and your emotional state at the time, you will find out when you are tempted to stray from your plan, which is the key to changing unhelpful behaviour.

'You'd be surprised at how emotional you can feel during the weight-loss journey,' says trainer Michelle Bridges. 'I would definitely recommend using a journal as you will start to see a pattern in what you are feeling. Often it can be a real roller-coaster ride so it is fantastic if you have an outlet for your emotions.'

After writing in your daily journal for a while you will see a pattern emerging, revealing when you are most vulnerable to temptations. Perhaps it's when you arrive home from work after a long day and feel the need to 'reward' yourself with a glass of wine and a kilojoule-heavy snack, or maybe it's late in the afternoon at work when you feel the snack-vending machine calling your name. In some cases you may feel the desire to indulge in high-kilojoule, high-carbohydrate foods after arguing with someone close. Recording every morsel you eat and the correlating situation allows you to take stock and make some positive changes.

If, for instance, you identify that your problem times are likely to arise when socialising with friends, you may suggest to them that you opt for an energising walk rather than meeting at a cafe.

As *The Biggest Loser* contestants found, documenting what you eat is one of the most helpful things you can do. In fact, according to one of the largest and longest-running weight-loss trials, conducted by the Kaiser Permanente Center for Health Research, keeping a food diary will not only make you more aware of your habits and change your behaviour, it can actually double your weight-loss results!

BIGGEST LOSER BIG TIP

'Keeping a food diary is essential.'

Write down what you eat each day. This includes all food and fluids – it is vital to record everything that goes into your mouth. This way you get to see where you can improve, and can also pinpoint trouble spots. The other great thing you can do is to buy a calorie counting book so you can educate yourself on the calorie content of the foods you eat.

Adro Sarnelli, Season 1

SAMPLE FOOD DIARY

What kind?	How much?	Time?	Where?	Alone or with whom?	Activity?	Mood?	Thoughts?	Thoughts for next time?

How much?
Write the quantity and kilojoule content of the particular food item you ate.

E.g., 2 cookies. Approx 1020 kj in total.

Time?
Write the time of day you ate the food.

E.g., 3.30 pm.

Where?
Write what room or part of the house you were in when you ate. If you ate in a restaurant, office, on the go or in your car, write down that location.

E.g., I got the cookies from the snack-vending machine in the staff kitchen, and ate one as I was walking back to my office and the other at my desk.

Alone or with whom?
If you ate by yourself, write 'alone'. If you were with friends, colleagues or family members, note who they were.

E.g., Alone.

Activity?
In this column, list any activities you were doing while you were eating. Perhaps you were working, watching TV, studying, preparing meals or socialising.

E.g., Had just come out of a stressful marketing meeting and arrived back at desk to numerous messages and emails.

Mood?
How were you feeling while you were eating? Were you sad, anxious, angry, happy or depressed?

E.g., Feeling overwhelmed, stressed.

Thoughts?
What thoughts were running through your mind as you ate?

E.g., Wondering how I will get it all done. There is all too much, it's overwhelming. I need a break.

Thoughts for next time?
This is where you can put cognitive behaviour techniques to work. Consider if there is a more helpful way to view the situation.

E.g., It helps if I tackle it step by step and break it down into manageable pieces. I will schedule a meeting with my boss to discuss ways we can delegate some of this work. It's not the end of the world – it is just work and definitely not worth compromising my health for. I do the best job I can and that's all anyone can do. Perhaps I just need to step outside and clear my head for a while. I will plan some pleasurable activities a few nights after work this week to allow me to regain a healthier perspective and keep me feeling happy.

Overcoming Cravings

One of the greatest challenges *The Biggest Loser* contestants face is finding alternative ways to occupy themselves when cravings strike.

The solution is sticking to those foods that will help you achieve your weight-loss goals, and making sure you find things to do instead of turning to sugary or fatty food for comfort. It takes time for your body to become accustomed to new, healthy eating habits, but stick it out – your perseverance will be rewarded!

When a craving does occur, try not to panic. Instead, acknowledge your feelings and then act differently from how you would have in the past. 'Cravings are only as strong as you let them be,' advises Adro Sarnelli, Season 1. 'Reaching for junk food is simply a habit and habits can be broken. I tell myself that I am in control and choose to do something else.'

At times your cravings may seem overwhelming. When this happens, turn to your food diary and write down what is going on in your life at that exact time. By reading your food journal regularly you will start to recognise triggers for your cravings and learn how to combat them. And remember: cravings pass! By employing the 'delay and distract' technique outlined earlier, you can move on and invest your time and energy in something productive.

If you do find yourself reaching for a 'hit', always go for the healthy option. Instead of indulging in a high-fat sugary snack, try an apple or a small portion of fruit salad.

BIGGEST LOSER BIG TIP

'I've learnt to control my cravings.'

Before appearing on *The Biggest Loser*, it was standard for Munnalita to devour a family-size block of chocolate each night, as well as half a loaf of bread. 'I was a huge bread, pasta, potatoes and chocolate eater,' she concedes. 'I ate whatever I wanted without really thinking about the consequences. Now I am a lot more aware and make choices that will benefit me in the long term. If I feel a craving coming on I usually do something to distract myself, like go for a walk. If I feel like I really have to have something, I opt for a black coffee or a diet soft drink that satisfies my sweet tooth. I also drink a lot of water, which really helps keep cravings at bay.'

Munnalita Kyrimis, Season 2

Learn to Say 'No'

One of the most important and empowering things you can do when losing weight is mastering the art of saying 'no'.

Many overweight people realise that one reason they have let the kilos creep on is simply because they didn't make their health a priority. Loving yourself means taking the time to look after yourself. It also means accepting who you are and acknowledging that you deserve the best life possible.

For Garry Guerreiro, Season 3, making his health a priority meant learning to be more assertive with friends. 'Before the show I had a group of mates whose catch-ups were always based around food. We would go to the pub for a feed or end up at a fast-food joint like Maccas or KFC. After I left the show I realised the damage this was doing and had to take a stand and just say no.'

'Putting myself first was probably the hardest thing I learnt to do,' agrees Adro Sarnelli, Season 1. 'The Biggest Loser taught me how. Suddenly I was the only person I had to worry about and it enabled me to get strong. You actually help others by helping yourself.'

By valuing yourself and projecting a confident self-image you will command respect and attention from others. In his book *Psycho-Cybernetics*, Dr Maxwell Maltz theorised that our self-image dictates the level of our success. So every time you are faced with doubts or are tempted to put someone else's needs before your health, stop and simply say 'no'.

The picture we have of ourselves not only affects our own life but also has a serious effect on our loved ones. According to research conducted by the Department of Psychology at the University of Potsdam in Germany, children of overweight parents bear a greater risk of being overweight themselves. When you look after your own needs and feelings first, you also set a healthy example for those around you. If you prioritise your health you will become a stronger, more vital and energetic person, and your family will benefit.

BIGGEST LOSER BIG TIP

If you get the craving for something, wait for 30 minutes. Just walk away and do something else for a while. If you are still obsessing about it later, permit yourself to have a small portion. If it's chocolate, for example, don't eat the whole block – instead have a couple of pieces. Allow yourself the odd treat. You may want to nominate certain times when you can splash out, like pasta on Sunday for lunch, or a small dessert. The important thing is to limit yourself to once a week. The key is control.

Courtney Jackson, Season 3

ALISON

PREVIOUS WEIGHT

121.7

CURRENT WEIGHT

114.9

DIFFERENCE

-6.8

BIGGEST LOSER BIG TIP

My view on what's important has really changed since being on the show. These days the ironing pile is just that little bit higher, but it doesn't matter because I will have gone for an invigorating run instead. Having time just for me is far more important these days. I believe that by being a strong and confident individual you are actually being a far better role model for your children. They see you getting out there and living your life and it teaches them to become strong and confident kids.

Alison Braun, Season 3

7 EASY WAYS TO EAT RIGHT

1 Practise conscious eating
Make meal times sacred. Set the table, light candles at dinner and savour the occasion. Always sit down when you are eating and chew food slowly. Leave time between mouthfuls and stop to rest every now and then. Dieticians advise leaving half an hour to properly enjoy your meal. ✓

2 Eat breakfast
As the saying goes, 'Eat breakfast like a king, lunch like a prince and dinner like a pauper.' By eating a good healthy breakfast you put enough fuel in your tank to boost your metabolism and get you on your way. ✓

3 Practise portion control
It's not only what you eat that counts but how much. Know your daily kilojoule budget and stick to the correct portions throughout the day. ✓

4 Drink water
Before reaching for food, realise that you may just be thirsty. Drink at least eight glasses of water each day to keep feeling hydrated and full. ✓

5 Eliminate alcohol, 'white' foods and junk foods
These all induce cravings and are full of 'empty kilojoules'. ✓

6 Write it down
Curb emotional eating by keeping a food diary. Have a set of alternative activities on standby and abstain from eating late at night. ✓

7 Just say no
Learn to pass up unhealthy foods and you're on the way to thinking and acting like a fit person. ✓

Relax

To maintain vibrant health and lose weight effectively, stress management is essential! If you use food as a way to alleviate feelings of stress or anxiety, it is time to build some healthier coping mechanisms into your life.

Activities such as yoga or Pilates lower stress and increase insulin sensitivity, which encourages your body to burn food as fuel rather than store it as fat. Both of these workouts promote flexibility, balance, focus and concentration and can be a helpful supplement to your regular exercise routine.

Likewise, deep breathing is a fantastic way to relax by restoring oxygen to the blood and boosting energy levels. Simply find somewhere quiet, close your eyes and take ten deep breaths. Do this three times a day and the results may surprise you!

Developing the daily habit of relaxing your mind and focusing on your goals will help you retain clarity, perspective and ultimately aid your weight loss. So the next time you are feeling stressed – stop, count to ten and BREATHE!

Carrianne Rees, Season 3, says, 'Running is my form of meditation. I just zone out and enjoy the surroundings. I particularly like running at sunrise or sunset. I try and change it around every time so I've always got something new to take in. I find it really relaxing.'

Toughest Moment:
Carrianne Rees, Season 3

There was a day when our trainer had us on the treadmills, sweating away, and then she abruptly stopped us and sat us down. She ordered us to say something good about ourselves in front of the rest of the team. People started coming up with things straight away but when my turn came I couldn't think of anything.

It was really confronting because for the first time I was being forced to think about myself in the positive rather than the negative. I ended up crying my eyes out because I found the whole exercise really hard.

It was difficult admitting to myself and everyone else in the group that I couldn't think of one worthwhile attribute, but more than anything I hated feeling so exposed. I had always put on a real front and allowed myself to come across as very confident, but now they knew the truth. I felt extremely vulnerable because I had let down my mask and revealed that I wasn't as strong as everybody thought.

Best Moment:
Tracy Moores, Season 1

I loved the camaraderie I shared with two of the other contestants. No-one really understands what it's like being on the show so it's great to have these people who were with you all the way and who went through the same experience. We were there for each other 100 per cent and have remained best mates ever since.

Munnalita's Moment of Revelation

My moment of revelation came one afternoon when I had the chance to eliminate a contestant from the Blue Team. My competitive streak kicked in and I decided it would be a girl who could possibly win or take me out later. I thought, 'It's not nice but it's something that has to be done.' The girl I had chosen to eliminate was like me, in that I noticed she also had big legs. Suddenly it dawned on me that if I was eliminated that day, I probably wouldn't be able to keep losing the weight. I asked myself, 'How would I like it if that was me and I was eliminated?'

For the rest of the afternoon I felt really emotional, and I ended up at the fridge. There was nothing fattening there so I pulled out a couple of lite chocolate mousses, which were the only treats we were allowed in the house. I sat there and gulped them both down.

Then it hit me that I was in a weight-loss house, surrounded by all the resources I needed to lose weight, and yet my eating was still out of control. I was shovelling more and more into my mouth. There wasn't any junk food in the house but I was still bingeing: it was the process of putting food in my mouth that I was used to. It was an emotional problem I needed to fix.

I did a lot of thinking and spoke to my trainer Michelle. Eating was the way I coped with emotional upsets. When some people reach breaking point they go for a cigarette; others reach for a glass of wine. For me it was food. I would go to the fridge or the cupboard or grab the car keys to drive myself down to the shops so I could buy food to eat. I realised that you could put me in a house for a year with the best trainers in the world, but at the end of it, if I hadn't tackled the underlying problem, the weight was likely to come back on.

It was like putting an alcoholic in an alcohol-free zone: if you don't treat the cause, they will only start drinking again later on.

Michelle asked me what I could have done instead of eating and I honestly didn't know. She drilled me again and again, asking, 'What could you have done?'

Suddenly I realised how different my life would be if, in that moment of crisis, I did something else rather than eat. When the emotions hit me, what if, rather than putting food in my mouth, I pulled on my sneakers, walked out the door and went around the block? By the time I came back home the emotions would have subsided, I would have calmed down and everything would be okay.

It was obvious that my coping mechanism was actually part of the problem. If I had chosen to walk rather than to eat, I would never have put the weight on in the first place. This revelation changed everything. For the first time I realised I had the power to choose my response and it completely turned things around.

Munnalita Kyrimis, Season 2

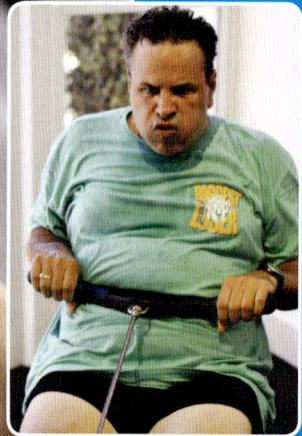

3

Exercise: Move Your Way to Success!

The slimmest and healthiest people in life are generally those who are the most active. On *The Biggest Loser*, contestants are taught the importance of incorporating exercise into their daily life and moving on a regular basis.

Aside from guaranteeing you'll shed kilos, regular exercise has many other benefits. These include:

▶ **Increased stamina and energy levels:** As well as boosting your metabolism, exercise energises you, leaving you feeling stimulated and refreshed. Having higher levels of energy encourages you to move more, which in turn makes losing weight even easier!

Better sleep: Exercise is a well-known sleep enhancer. Research shows that doing approximately 45 minutes of cardiovascular exercise most days (such as jogging, swimming, cycling, aerobics or spin class) will improve your sleep.

Elevated mood: Studies have shown that exercise alters the body's biochemistry. By releasing pleasure-inducing brain chemicals called endorphins, physical activity can provide the pleasurable feelings you might previously have obtained from eating. Being active makes you feel happier!

Lower stress levels: Numerous studies show that people who exercise regularly are less stressed than those who don't. Physical activity provides you with a dose of feel-good endorphins while also allowing you to gain valuable perspective.

Improved immunity: The average adult contracts two to three upper respiratory infections each year. One of the most effective ways to prevent ill health is to build moderate, regular exercise into your lifestyle. Training consistently helps boost your immune system and people who exercise report fewer colds and viruses than those who don't.

BIGGEST LOSER BIG TIP

My advice is to make exercise a priority and slot it into your day no matter what. Make sure it's something you enjoy so you don't see it as a chore. Treat your training sessions as an opportunity to escape for an hour and make it something just for you.

Alison Braun, Season 3

As trainer Shannan Ponton says, 'Exercise is everything! If you want to get fitter and healthier, lose weight and lead a better life, it is essential you establish a structured exercise program.' Trainer Michelle agrees. 'Consistent exercise is the key to feeling great, losing weight and keeping it off. Every little bit counts, so take every opportunity you can to move.'

It takes motivation and discipline to stick to an exercise regimen, but take heart: once you begin, it does get easier. By following the advice of the Biggest Losers and trainers Shannan and Michelle, you will enjoy the substantial benefits from training regularly. This chapter is full of tips to get you on your way.

Make Exercise a Priority

The first thing to do is make exercise your number one priority. Follow the advice of experts and ensure that nothing gets in your way.

Trainer Michelle Bridges believes the best way to start is to 'get your exercise out of the way as soon as you can each day. I mostly train in the morning: that way I don't blow it off if I get busy later on. Once it's done, it's done, and I can get into other things. As a personal trainer, exercise will always be a big priority but it should also be a high priority for everyone else who wants to get into shape. You have to constantly revisit your priorities and ask "How badly do I want this?" and make time to exercise every day.'

Likewise, trainer Shannan Ponton 'walks the talk' when it comes to training. 'My training is always locked in,' he declares. 'For me, it is the priority and if I miss my exercise then everything else suffers. When I miss a training session I'm not as quick, I'm not as astute and I feel really disappointed with myself. Exercise empowers you to function at a much higher level in all aspects of your life.'

A great way to step up your activity is to buy a pedometer. Put it on first thing in the morning and plan to walk 10,000 steps every day. If you find you are under your daily requirement, you can then compensate by either cutting back on your kilojoule intake or boosting your activity level.

Courtney Jackson, Season 2, advises: 'Just get out and move! Go for a walk or run. Once you get started, it gets the ball rolling and you will eventually learn to love exercise. We were made to be active, not sedentary. You start to sleep better, you have better moods, you feel happy and healthy, and then you start to see results, which you'll love even more! Exercise will change your body in ways that diet alone never can. You'll tone up, develop better reflexes and feel great. Exercise enhances your life in every conceivable way.'

One of the great advantages of training regularly is that it encourages what is known as the 'afterburn effect', that is, the body's ability to continue burning kilojoules even after you have stopped exercising. When you exercise and gain more muscle your body effectively becomes a fat-burning machine, because muscle requires more kilojoules to maintain than fat. Exercise will speed up your metabolism, increasing your energy expenditure above its normal capacity. You'll begin to lose weight even when you aren't working out.

SHANNAN SAYS

It all comes down to commitment and being true to yourself. If you really want the results, there's nobody else who can get them for you. You have to take responsibility for your life and for achieving your goals. If you're a millionaire you can't pay someone else to train for you. There's no easy way around it, there is no trick. You have to decide that you want to do it and realise you deserve it. Exercise is the key to leading a happier and healthier life.

Develop a More Active Lifestyle

One of the most significant shifts you'll have to make is to start thinking and acting like a fit person. Fit and healthy people find excuses to move, so aim to increase your activity quota in your everyday life.

Aside from your scheduled workouts at the gym and daily training sessions, start by asking yourself, 'How can I increase my physical activity at other times of the day?'

BIGGEST LOSER BIG TIP

One of the best bits of advice I was given on the show was 'don't stop moving'. Move whenever you can. Instead of watching TV, get up and go for a walk or a bike ride. Rather than sitting around and chatting, hop on the treadmill. To lose weight you need to do the opposite of what you've been doing for all these years. Swap a sedentary life for an active life.

Adro Sarnelli, Season 1

By increasing your physical activity you will find you have more energy and vitality to complete everyday tasks. The more you do, the more you want to do. Over the course of a day, incidental exercise can really add up and help shift those kilos!

MICHELLE SAYS

Intensity is king, so if you can develop a sweat on your brow and be huffing and puffing, you know your training regimen is working for you. Anything from running to climbing stairs to doing a circuit is great! You might begin being able to run up only one flight of stairs, but over the next few weeks that will increase to three flights, and then five, and eventually you'll make it to ten. Keep pushing yourself and raising the bar!

Vary Your Routine

To optimise your results, it helps to vary your exercise program. Your body requires a combination of cardio and muscle-building exercises to burn fat efficiently, so it is best to alternate aerobic activity such as jogging, spin classes and cycling with resistance training such as push-ups, sit-ups and workouts with weights.

A typical program will involve:

▶ **Cardiovascular exercise:** 3 times per week for 45 minutes per session. This is the best way to rev up your metabolism, help burn fat and strengthen your heart and lungs. Activities might include high-speed walking, jogging, running, swimming, skipping, cycling, spin classes, aerobic classes, rockclimbing, hiking, dance classes, tennis, soccer, football, netball or basketball.

▶ **Strength training:** 2 times per week for 45 minutes per session. This is the best way to build and maintain muscle as well as prevent bone-deteriorating conditions such as osteoporosis. Activities might include any type of weight-training involving dumbbells or weight machines. You may also wish to incorporate exercises where you use your own body weight as a form of resistance, such as sit-ups, push-ups, chin-ups or squats.

Adro Sarnelli, Season 1, says, 'The best way to get fit and lose weight is through interval training. Variety really is the spice of life! The more you train, the more momentum you gain and the easier it is to keep going. Once motivation comes from within, you become virtually unstoppable.'

'Variety is definitely the key,' agrees Kirsten Binnie, Season 3. 'I always try and mix my training sessions up as much as possible. One day I do a spin class, the next I run on the treadmill, then the day after that I do an aerobics class. Sometimes I won't go to the gym at all – instead, if it's a nice day, I'll go for a walk or run outdoors.'

SHANNAN SAYS

Incidental exercise really helps! Try walking up a few flights of stairs in your building instead of taking the lift. Do this four or five times a day and it will make a difference. Park your car further away from the station and walk, take the dog for a run when you get home from work, or take your kids down to the park and kick a ball. Whatever it is, just get moving and active. Build this into your daily life on top of your structured exercise regimen and you will soon see results.

Make it Fun!

One of the best ways to ensure you stick to your fitness regimen is to have fun! This might mean joining a team or combining social activity with your training workout.

Bryce Harvey, Season 3, observes, 'You're not going to stick to an exercise routine unless you genuinely enjoy what you are doing. So if you're a person who likes swimming, go and join a swimming club or find an ocean pool and do some laps.

Personally I love team sports so I play footy – we train during the week and play games every Saturday. Because I love it, it doesn't feel like exercise, it's just fun.'

Be creative and do things you never thought you would do – join a bushwalking club and take in the sights, try kayaking or dragon boat racing, join a soccer team, enrol in dance classes, go hiking or rock climbing, or start up taekwondo. Extend yourself, stimulate your senses, and embark on new challenges and quests.

BIGGEST LOSER BIG TIP

Do something you enjoy! The key is to keep it interesting. If you love dancing then go and do a salsa class or some ballroom dancing. It's an extra hour in your week where you are out and about and moving around, rather than sitting on your couch. If you do the things you enjoy then exercise doesn't feel like a chore.

Kirsten Binnie, Season 3

Enlist Some Expert Help

Recruit some professional help to get you started. Even if you only do a few sessions with a personal trainer, it will give you an idea of the type of exercise that is best for you and the correct amount of repetitions needed to lose weight.

Having to report to a trainer will also keep you accountable and prevent you from bailing out of your sessions.

Courtney Jackson, Season 2, agrees. 'I would highly recommend getting a personal trainer,' he says, 'whether it's once a week, once a fortnight or once a month. Trainers will motivate you and teach you what to do. One idea is to pay a trainer to write a program for you and then take you through it. It is a worthwhile investment in your health and future! Maintaining a healthy lifestyle is vital and you simply can't afford not to look after yourself. Classes in gyms are also fantastic. The instructors create a fun atmosphere with lots of great music so it's over before you know it!'

As any Biggest Loser will tell you, you have to 'move it to lose it!'

Burning more kilojoules than you consume is the secret behind losing weight, so if you remember 'kilojoules in = kilojoules out' and burn off what you eat, you are ensuring that you stay trim and terrific for life.

SHANNAN SAYS

A personal trainer will show you the correct exercises to do and then you can go off by yourself for the next few weeks. It may be enough just to touch base once a month or so. To get the correct information and expertise in the initial stages is vital. That way you will know the most effective workout techniques from the beginning, which will ultimately help you lose weight and get toned. By consulting a fitness professional you will get the results you deserve.

SHANNAN'S TOP TRAINING TIPS FOR MEN

1 Big is not always better

Don't think that lifting heavy weights is always going to be the key!

2 Balance your training

Many guys get into the gym and do bench press and bicep curls and forget about the other important bits (like their back and legs) and can end up looking like a crab. Make sure all your muscles get an even workout.

3 Never forget cardiovascular training

Heart disease is the number one killer of men. Males typically store their fat around their torso, which is detrimental to your heart health. You must maintain a good cardiovascular training regimen to keep your heart and lungs healthy.

4 Vary your training

The best workouts involve a variety of different components with a mixture of cardio and weights. A great idea is to mix up your gym workouts with some form of competitive sport. Try basketball, touch football or soccer. Anything with an air of competition is fantastic as it often seems to bring the best out in males.

MICHELLE'S TOP TRAINING TIPS FOR WOMEN

1 It's all in the mind

Most of the time when you are tempted to stop it's simply your head making excuses. Sure, your body is probably tired and hurting a bit but that's completely normal. If you can talk yourself through it you will be surprised at what you can achieve.

2 Intensity is king

If your token gesture is going for a stroll around the block with a girlfriend, you can't expect great results. You need to be working yourself to the point where you feel out of breath. Try jogging for 20 minutes or pushing yourself in a spin class.

3 Be consistent

Make sure you do something most days of the week. I would recommend training Monday through to Saturday then taking a rest day on Sunday.

4 Mix it up

I advise women to do some form of cardiovascular training interspersed with weight-bearing exercises.

5 Enjoy yourself!

If you don't enjoy what you are doing it makes it harder to stick with it. If you find exercising is getting to be a bore, go and try a fitness or dance class.

Toughest Moment:
Bryce Harvey, Season 3

One of the toughest things is learning to override the voice in your head. It will try to convince you that because you've had a hard day, you deserve some junk food. You have to be strong and talk back to that voice: 'No! What are you doing? Why would you even consider going back to those old habits? Remember how bad you used to feel about yourself?' It takes time but gradually you get the hang of it!

Best Moment:
Garry Guerreiro, Season 3

My best moment was during a training session. The longest time I had run on the treadmill previously was for 5 minutes, but on this particular day I got on and ran nonstop for 20 minutes. It felt incredible. When I stopped, my team-mates got off their equipment and applauded me.

4

The Inner Journey: Be Focused, Positive and Strong

Now is the time for you to shed unwanted kilos, spread your wings and become the person you have always wanted to be!

As you lose weight, you will feel increasingly confident and hopeful about your future, which will in turn play a fundamental part in helping you reach your goals.

Everyone has difficult days – those times when you doubt yourself and the trek seems hard. Perhaps you are comparing yourself to unrealistic 'ideals' as displayed in the media, or engaging in negative self-talk. At these moments you must remain focused, develop your inner resolve and master the art of self-love.

In this chapter *The Biggest Loser* cast members discuss their inner journeys and the ways they learnt to love their bodies, honour their individual paths and stay motivated, positive and strong.

Be Your Own Best Friend

It is a fact of life that others will not respect you until you love and respect yourself. Part of loving yourself means accepting who you are right now and forgiving any perceived imperfections. As Martin Luther King said, 'Forgiveness is not an occasional act; it is a permanent attitude.'

Many people have a belief deep down inside that they are unworthy or don't deserve true happiness. They find ways to confirm this belief and inadvertently sabotage themselves from obtaining the life they deserve. If this sounds like you, it's time to ask yourself where these negative thoughts stem from.

'When I first entered the house I didn't actually believe I could lose the weight,' confesses Courtney Jackson, Season 2. 'I felt useless and was convinced I wasn't strong enough. As the weeks went on and the kilos slipped away, something inside me clicked – I realised that I COULD do it. My entire focus changed from "I can't do it and I'm useless" to "I can do it and I'm worth it!" '

Health, as defined by the World Health Organization, is 'a state of complete physical, mental and social wellbeing, and not merely the absence of disease.' Optimum health is your birthright: you should have the energy, vitality and conviction to pursue your dreams and live your best life. As philosopher Elbert Hubbard said, 'If you have health

you are probably happy, and if you have health and happiness, you have all the wealth you need.'

'It is very common for women in particular to put everything else before their own needs,' comments trainer Michelle Bridges. 'So often they worry about their kids, their husbands, their household and job and have so many different things to balance that they forget how important it is to put themselves first. If you make yourself number one then you are actually able to give a lot more.'

If you are merely surviving, rather than thriving, now is the time to make amends. The first thing you can do is acknowledge the relationship between your mental and physical state: accept that your body is simply a reflection of how you feel about yourself. Life is what your thoughts make it, so if you are constantly beating yourself up, this is likely to manifest itself in your appearance. It is vital to believe you deserve to be healthy and that it is your right to excel and shine in life, and not just make it through.

Adro Sarnelli, Season 1, says, 'The most significant lesson I learnt throughout the entire *Biggest Loser* experience was the importance of believing in yourself. If you don't love yourself, other people can't love you either, because you will unconsciously push them away.'

Learn to be your own best friend. Nurture yourself by pampering your body through non-food activities and be determined never to say another negative thing about yourself again. If you have spent years telling yourself you are not good enough, or you have no right to the life you truly want, this will take practice. But if you commit to an attitude of self-respect, slowly but surely you will see results.

MICHELLE SAYS

Take some time out each day to just sit quietly. Go through your goals and ask yourself what you want to achieve. Focus not just on the physical, but also on the fact you want to be around for a long time so you can enjoy your family. Rather than dwelling on the dress size you want to be, think about how much you want to be there for your children. This encourages you to have balance in your life and means your goals are long-lasting.

Munnalita Kyrimis, Season 2, explains, 'When I first went into the house I wasn't feeling very good about myself. But as the weeks progressed and I lost some weight I gained a little more confidence. I would stand in front of the mirror and say, "Oh, you're coming along quite nicely!" and would make a real effort to feel better about myself.'

As Munnalita discovered, words are power! The words we use determine how we feel about ourselves and dictate our subsequent actions. It may help to write down some affirming thoughts on cards and keep them in your wallet or purse, or attach them to the sun visor in your car or on your mirror at home. Recite them whenever you can.

Some useful affirmations are:

▶ **I have unlimited potential, I believe in me!**

▶ **I can accomplish anything!**

▶ **I love being me.**

▶ **I am beautiful, lean, healthy and strong and move towards my dreams every day.**

▶ **I love and nurture myself, knowing I deserve the best life possible.**

▶ **I nourish myself from within.**

▶ **I focus on my strengths; I am my own best friend.**

BIGGEST LOSER BIG TIP

As mums, it often feels like we are the ones holding the family together. As a result we allow our needs to sit right down the bottom of the list while we look after everyone else. It shouldn't be this way. Children follow their parents' example, so the best thing we can do is take some time out and care for ourselves. It is important to show your kids you respect yourself so they can learn to do that too.

Tracy Moores, Season 1

It may also be beneficial to question the images you see on TV or in magazines. All too often we are faced with unrealistic portrayals of what men and women 'should' look like, when in fact no two bodies are the same. Rather than viewing exercise as a tool to become 'Barbie thin', focus on building a lean, strong and healthy body.

Experts agree that even if we all ate the same healthy diet and did the same amount of exercise, everyone would still have a different body shape – some quite big, some thin, but mostly in between. Accept that you have your own unique shape, and make the most of yourself by exercising regularly and nourishing your body with great healthy fuel!

Pati and the Affirmation

Throughout the show I constantly had debates inside my head. I found that my old negative thoughts would creep in and tell me that I was essentially unlovable, I wasn't worth it and no amount of hard work was going to make a difference.

The old Pati would say, 'It doesn't matter how much weight you lose. No-one is ever going to want you because you are such a closed-off person and you have lived as a hermit for the last 26 years. How are they ever going to get to know and appreciate the real you?'

The truth is I really wanted a better life and to share it with a partner. I wanted to be with someone I could be totally open with and someone who would love me completely for the person I am inside.

One of the trainers pointed out that the thing holding me back was my thoughts. It took me a while but I began to replace the negative voices with something positive. So whenever I heard myself say, 'No-one will want you', I replaced it with, 'I am getting there, I am learning to love myself and realise I deserve more.' It dawned on me that you need to appreciate yourself first before anyone else can get close.

It was a matter of catching my negative thoughts and reframing what I was saying to myself. I told myself how good I felt and slowly but surely it started to ring true. I began to believe that someone worthwhile would come along who would be prepared to invest time and love in me.

It actually worked out quite well because I now have a lovely partner and we are expecting a baby. I'm over the moon!

Pati Singe, Season 2

Be Realistic

If you are like the majority of people carrying excess weight, those extra kilos most likely crept on over the years. Changing behaviour isn't easy and it's going to take a while to get used to your healthy new routines.

Change in life is gradual. Not only are you altering the way you eat and move, you are also making inner adjustments, such as reassessing your existing thought patterns. It helps if you commit yourself to your goal and make small but meaningful steps towards your targets every day.

Adro Sarnelli, Season 1, agrees. 'It took a lot of time getting to be the weight you were, and it will take time getting it off again. Start putting in the time and effort and you will gradually lose weight, rather than gaining more. It *is* possible to reverse the process.'

BIGGEST LOSER BIG TIP

Change takes time. The key is never to give up. Even when it's tough going you need to remind yourself you are worth fighting for and that it will take time and effort. When your progress seems slow you have to realise that you are doing a lot better than before. Every little bit counts and it all adds up in the long run. Don't think of how far you have to go, focus on what you have already achieved!

Courtney Jackson, Season 2

Michelangelo described sculpture as a process of removing excess marble that covered the beauty of the figure within. So, too, you are sculpting a new creation from your former self. It requires endurance and persistence, but if you stick with it you will see beautiful results from all your hard work.

Of course this will not happen overnight, but if you set realistic goals for yourself and celebrate each step along the way, the time-consuming process of unveiling the real you becomes easier.

BIGGEST LOSER BIG TIP

Every person's journey is different. Some people will find exercise easier, others will find changing their diet and eliminating certain foods really easy. Some will lose weight quickly and then plateau, while others might struggle initially and gain momentum later on. Work out how your body responds and devise the system that is best for you. You might find that having six or seven small meals is the key, while someone else will be better off with three. Some of us need to do high-intensity exercise, but others are better off with low intensity. You may have to try a lot of different things before you work out how your body functions and the best way for you to lose weight.

Kirsten Binnie, Season 3

Focus on Your Strengths

One of the winning formulas for leading a successful life is recognising that every individual has their own set of gifts and strengths. It is up to you to find out what yours are, and then to use them.

What you focus on seems to expand, so if you pay attention to your strengths, negative behaviour and unwanted patterns will fall away. If you focus on what makes you feel happy and fulfilled, chances are you won't use food or your old unhealthy habits to fill a void. By honouring your talents you will nourish from the INSIDE, which is the catalyst for dramatic, positive and permanent change.

To identify your strengths, simply ask, 'When do I feel most present, focused, clear and strong?' Are there activities that, when you embark on them, make you lose track of time? Successful people focus on success. They capitalise on what they want and what makes them feel great. They use their abilities to benefit themselves and their communities and dwell on the positive aspects of their character. They know that each of us is responsible for creating our own life through every thought, action and choice, and they acknowledge the importance of choosing wisely.

Marcus Buckingham, author and acclaimed strength-training coach, recommends focusing on what makes you special. 'If you want to know what your strength is, you've got to pay attention to how you feel. It feels like focus. It feels like concentration. You feel invigorated. Energised.'

Take a step back and analyse your current lifestyle or job. Are you feeling fulfilled on a daily basis, or are you searching for something else to 'fill you up'? If you are a social and communicative person, for example, and you have a job that is mainly isolated and desk-bound, you may find that changing jobs or immersing yourself in an engaging new hobby helps.

The laws of attraction state that what you consistently focus on becomes your reality. If you feel alive, excited, purposeful and strong, that in turn attracts even more positivity into your life. You owe it to yourself to honour your originality, to invest in your talents, work hard and believe good things will happen for you.

'One of the things I did throughout my weight-loss journey was to visualise how life would be once I lost the weight,' says Carrianne Rees, Season 3. 'The most powerful thing I could imagine was hanging out with my family and friends, being happy and having a wonderful time. I saw myself as feeling relaxed, in control and confident within myself. Over time I actually began to feel more and more this way.'

Live an Authentic Life!

Real change happens from the inside out. Instead of dwelling on the exterior, you have to concentrate on the root cause of your problems: why have you previously chosen to be unhealthy? When outer choices reflect your inner desires, a sense of oneness or peace prevails and greater energy for healing becomes available. As many physicians and weight-loss experts agree, uncovering conflicts can be crucial to achieving this sense of peace within, which is essential to creating and maintaining happiness and health.

Leading an authentic life means being truthful with yourself and ensuring your actions reflect the person you are inside. As we have noted already, many *Biggest Loser* contestants previously used food as a way of ignoring unwanted feelings or the fact that there was something wrong in their life. By owning up to your problems and identifying your true needs, wants and desires, you can start to create a plan of action.

> ## BIGGEST LOSER BIG TIP
>
> It's imperative that you are honest with yourself. If you feel yourself slipping back to old habits, take responsibility for your actions and rein yourself in. Everyone knows when they are eating and drinking a bit much. When this happens, it's time to get your act together – cut out the alcohol and treats, and get more active in the gym.
>
> *Bryce Harvey, Season 3*

Garry Guerreiro, Season 3, concedes he is a more honest person after losing 70 kilograms. 'Before I entered the house I was pretty much at rock bottom and was hiding a lot of things – from myself and also the people around me. I was hiding behind my weight because I was embarrassed to let people know the real me. Now I make a point of being honest in my actions. If I say I will work out, then I do. Before, I used to make up all sorts of excuses, but now I hold myself accountable no matter what.'

Once you acknowledge your needs, you can address them. For example, if you feel lonely, rather than binge on fatty food, phone up a friend. If you are anxious, spend 10 minutes doing some relaxation exercises; if you are angry, go for a high-power run or do a boxing session at the gym. Ask yourself: 'How can this problem best be fixed?'

Banishing inner conflict from your life could be as simple as applying for a new job that uses your talents, making sure your outer actions correspond to your inner needs and dreams, or even just following through on what you say you will do.

Never underestimate the power of being authentic, expressing yourself as you truly are and allowing your inner self and spirit to shine through.

'Being authentic has become my entire way of being,' declares Adro Sarnelli, Season 1. 'In order for this to happen I first had to let go of the "old me". When I came out of *The Biggest Loser* house I had to change every facet of my daily existence because I was completely different from how I used to be. I used to work in the car industry but that was no longer relevant for me, so I changed careers and became a personal trainer. I realised very quickly that I needed a new life where I could use my knowledge and help others turn their lives around.'

Be Courageous

Sometimes in life we are presented with the opportunity to move forward but we cling to what we know because it's what we feel comfortable with. At times like this you need to be courageous.

Venturing away from your old unhealthy routines takes bravery. For many *Biggest Loser* contestants this means applying the 'fake it till you make it' principle – that is, establishing new patterns for yourself and finding alternative ways to feel good rather than relying on the temporary 'fix' obtained from food.

Eleanor Roosevelt said, 'You gain strength, courage, and confidence by every experience in which you really stop and look fear in the face . . . do the thing you think you cannot do.' So when you come home from work after a long, stressful day, rather than reaching for that high-kilojoule snack, extend yourself, put your best foot forward, pull on your running shoes and go forth into the world! Living your optimum life takes effort, commitment and courage, but if you heed the Biggest Losers you will see you CAN do it!

Trainer Michelle Bridges notes that it's often when you are losing weight and training hard that you feel emotionally raw. 'When people are training and feel exhausted, that's when emotion comes to the fore. But that's good, it's healthy, and that's the stuff we want to work through. It's the stuff that has been holding you back, that you've been suppressing. It's good to get it out into the open. It might mean just stopping and taking stock of what's been going on, or perhaps that you need to stop blaming others and take responsibility for yourself.'

Of course there are going to be moments when you feel discouraged and want to give in. But if you just keep the faith and stay true to your dream, you will discover a new strength emerges to keep you on track. By being your own best friend, taking care of yourself, having realistic expectations about your progress, focusing on your good points and living life as authentically as possible, you will set yourself up for the success you deserve.

SHANNAN SAYS

If you eat for emotional reasons, you have to drill it into your head that any positive feelings that result are very short-lived. You feel good for about 30 seconds and then terrible for the next 2 days because you've eaten something you shouldn't have and fallen off the wagon. It is important to remember how dreadful you feel afterwards, and how much you've let yourself down. Feeling fantastic and fit, strong and confident is far better than the taste of any food.

You can use your negative emotions to your advantage, so tap into that! Think of the times you felt embarrassed because of your weight: when you went on a plane and had to use an extender belt, or sat down and broke a chair. No amount of food could ever make up for those depressing feelings you experience when you are overweight.

Courtney Jackson, Season 2, recommends comparing how you felt before to how great you feel now. 'Do you want to feel miserable for the rest of your life? Do you want to settle for a lower quality of living? When you think of the pain of being overweight compared to the pain of physical exercise, they're not in the same league. It's crucial to recall the benefits of healthy living and how great you will feel when you finally arrive at your destination.'

As all the Biggest Losers know, real and lasting change comes from within, so commit yourself to the inner journey and enjoy the results!

BIGGEST LOSER BIG TIP

There are moments when it does get hard – your body is tired, you are mentally tired, or maybe you have simply had a bad week and haven't lost as much weight as you wanted. The easiest thing to do is to take some time out and remind yourself of your end goal. Perhaps it's to regain your confidence, to be happy again, or get back that twinkle in your eye. There were moments on the treadmill where I thought, 'I just want to stop, I want to get off,' but there was a picture on the wall of Adro, the Season 1 winner, on the scales at finale night, so I would look at that instead. I would visualise myself in the same position, standing up there in my dream dress. Just thinking about that made me happy again. When it all gets too hard, just visualise happiness for yourself and remind yourself of your goals.

Kirsten Binnie, Season 3

Toughest Moment:
Garry Guerreiro, Season 3

I found it really hard being away from all my family and friends. Initially I felt pretty lonely in the house but then I decided to turn things around. I thought, 'If I can't lose weight for myself then I will do it for the people I love.' I'd be on the treadmill and instead of focusing on the pain I would imagine how happy my father would be once I lost the weight.

Best Moment:
Alison Braun, Season 3

My best moment came when we went to Hawaii and faced our fears. I have an extreme fear of heights so my mission was to jump off a cliff into the sea. I felt sick because I knew I couldn't do it. I can't handle standing on a ledge, let alone jumping off one! It took a lot of coaxing from the trainers for me to even contemplate giving it a try. I was standing on the ledge saying, 'I can't do this, I can't do it.' Then I heard Shannan yell, 'Jump!' and so I gathered all my strength and leapt.

I hit the water pretty hard and was sinking down thinking, 'I'm never going to make it back up.' But when I resurfaced and took a breath of air it was like my very first breath of life. It felt like I was reborn.

I remember looking up from the ocean and realising I had just left my old life behind. Something clicked inside me and I've been different from that day on. One of the trainers commented later that night, 'There is a new sparkle in your eye,' and it's true. It was the start of my new life.

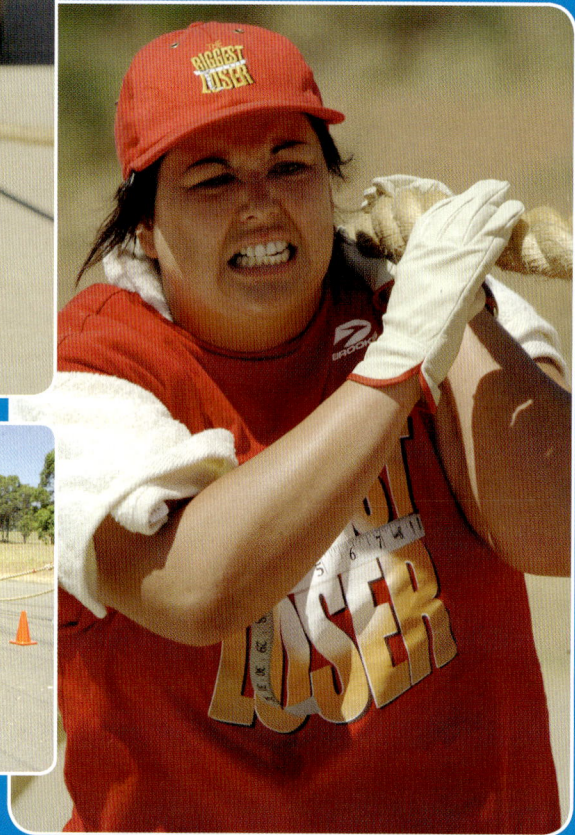

5
Keeping on Track

Maintaining motivation can be difficult and it's natural to feel discouraged from time to time. You may have to deal with a crisis, or you might lose the zest for working out or sticking to your healthy eating plan. Whatever happens, it's important to stay on track, which is sometimes easier said than done, but if you look at obstacles as opportunities and take pleasure in persevering you will come out on top.

Every cast member of *The Biggest Loser* has hit a brick wall at some stage and had to dig deep and find the strength to carry on. In this chapter they share how they found the determination to push on even in those moments when they felt they could not. They reveal their strategies for climbing what felt like insurmountable hurdles and losing kilos in the process. If you are struggling with your plan, read on and take heart from others who have been tested – and won.

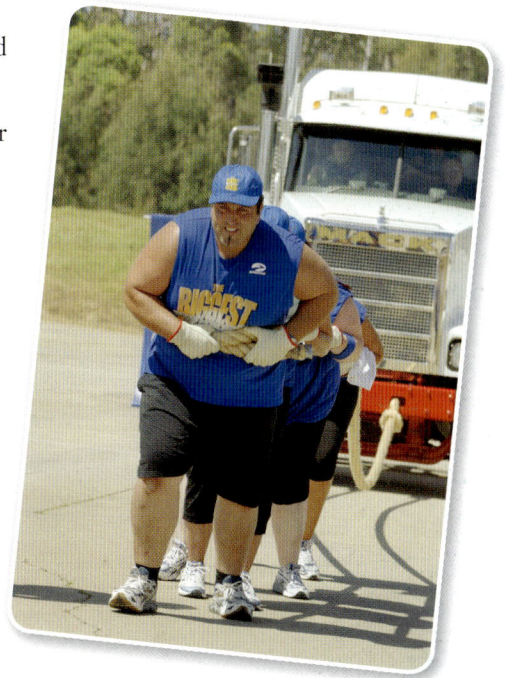

Write Down Your Goals

Successful businessman Henry Ford once said, 'Obstacles are those frightful things you see when you take your eyes off the goal.' Knowing what you want to achieve is your first step on the path to success. As the laws of attraction state, we gravitate towards what we think about most, so by having a list of goals you'd like to reach you can actually train your mind to move towards what you want.

By setting targets and working hard you begin to accept more responsibility for your future, which in turn gives you greater feelings of self-control. By making and keeping promises to yourself you will develop an inner strength and integrity that help build momentum and catapult you onwards.

The first thing to do is identify your goals. For some Biggest Losers this meant fitting into a pair of slimline jeans; for others it meant having the stamina to run around the park with their children or the confidence to pursue the dream of starting their own business.

Whatever you want, it is vital to write down your goals and desires.

Start by thinking of what your ideal future looks like. This becomes your broad vision or long-term goal. Ideally, these goals should cover all the important areas in your life, including health, career, family, finances, hobbies and so on. Next, identify any short-term goals that have specific relevance for you. In the case of the Biggest Losers this meant getting their health and wellbeing on track immediately.

Then separate your goals into smaller, realistic targets. When setting your health goals, for example, you could calculate your ideal weight, decide how you'd like to feel and what you will look like. Include any sporting or physical activities you'd like to participate in – things like mini marathons, or playing soccer or swimming with your kids.

BIGGEST LOSER BIG TIP

Be realistic and expect ups and downs along the way. Some weeks you lose a lot and some weeks you won't lose much at all. Stay focused on achieving small goals, one step at a time.

Kirsten Binnie, Season 3

According to experts, the best way to achieve your goals is by adhering to the SMART principal – that is, making your targets: specific, measurable, attainable, relevant and time-bound.

Specific: The best goals are clear and detailed. You should be able to decide whether you have reached a goal by asking yourself a 'yes or no' question. For instance, if your goal is 'lose ten kilos', you can ask yourself, 'Have I lost ten kilos yet?' When the answer is yes, you've reached your goal.

Measurable: Choose a figure. Decide the size or weight you would like to be, or the amount you want to lose. Vague goals, such as 'get in shape', can be discouraging, because it's hard to measure your progress towards them.

Attainable: Be realistic. You must have the capacity to reach your goals.

Relevant: Your objectives should be appropriate and meaningful to you. Plan to be fit enough to play soccer with your kids or go mountain climbing with your partner, rather than aiming to look like a size 8 waif in a magazine.

Time-bound: Set goals with a definite end point. Specify the time in which you plan to achieve them.

Let's consider an example. Rather than choosing 'I want to lose weight' as a goal, it is more powerful to say, 'I will lose 20 kilos within 5 months, and during that time I will also run a 10-kilometre mini marathon.' You then decide on an action plan, comprising a kilojoule-controlled diet, physical activity, relaxation and visualisation exercises, and the use of various psychological tools, such as journal-keeping and the 'delay and distract' technique. For every 5-kilo mini goal you reach, you should reward yourself – with a non-food item, of course!

As any top-level athlete or successful businessperson will attest, goal setting and writing is imperative to long-term success. By deciding where you would like to go, building a plan to get there, and putting it down on paper, you allow your vision to become reality.

BIGGEST LOSER BIG TIP

Make sure you reward yourself with things that aren't food-related. Perhaps you have just lost 5 kilograms – congratulations! Go out and buy yourself that pair of jeans you've had your eye on. Spoil yourself by going for a massage or facial or take yourself to the movies with friends.

Carrianne Rees, Season 3

Visualise Success

Once you have your goals written down you can maintain motivation by revisiting them daily and visualising how life will be once you reach them. Through your imagination you can create a whole new world for yourself.

Trainer Shannan Ponton advises that 'it comes down to being good to yourself' and knowing you deserve a better future. 'It's really hard to lose all that weight, so to revert back just doesn't do you justice. You have to constantly recall how great it feels to be in shape. Be strong, and determined to stay in control.'

Another of Henry Ford's famous sayings is: 'Whether you think you can, or think you can't – you are right!' Many world-class athletes, businesspeople and peak performers use visualisation to achieve the results they want. They see success, they feel it and they experience it *before it actually happens*. They refer to their goals constantly and live with a winner's mindset.

Spend 5 to 10 minutes each day replaying a 'movie' in your mind of how you'd like to look and how you'd like your life to be. The workings of the human brain are almost 90 per cent subconscious, and in our subconscious minds we cannot differentiate between an event we have visualised and one that has actually occurred. Therefore, if you consistently imagine yourself in a particular way, you'll begin to act and perform like that in everyday life. By implanting your goals into your subconscious and walking, talking and thinking like a lean, healthy and strong person, your outer being miraculously finds ways to fit this belief.

Place a copy of your goals everywhere you can and visualise them as though they have already happened. Whether you are standing in the kitchen in front of the fridge, driving in your car or at the mirror getting ready for work, let your mind play your special 'movie' where you see the healthy, fit you living the life you've always imagined!

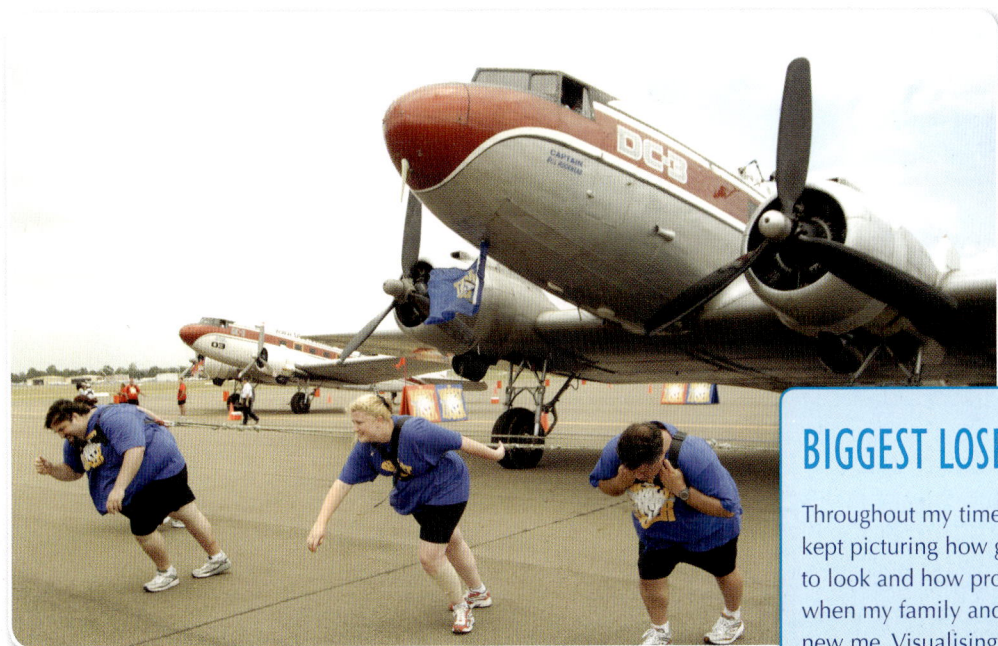

BIGGEST LOSER BIG TIP

Throughout my time on the show I kept picturing how good I was going to look and how proud I would feel when my family and friends saw the new me. Visualising success made me feel positive and kept me going in the tough times.

Munnalita Kyrimis, Season 2

Form New Habits

Aristotle said, 'We are what we repeatedly do. Excellence then is not an act, but a habit.' Habits are powerful forces in our lives that can be learned and unlearned at will. Establishing new habits takes time, though, and it is only through consistent effort that changes slowly become ingrained in your daily life. What you think, say and do dictates your future, so it's time to get this right!

This can be a painful process, particularly if you expect to see results overnight. In most cases, your existing eating patterns have been with you for years and it will take concerted application to make your new healthful routines instinctive. As you get going, though, it becomes easier, so take heart – every day is a step forward. Trainer Shannan Ponton notes, 'It comes down to strength and discipline. There is no clear-cut way of doing it other than being true to yourself, understanding yourself, knowing what your trigger situations are, then doing your best to avoid them. Be kind to yourself and don't throw yourself into situations where you know you'll be tempted.'

SHANNAN SAYS

It's important to weigh yourself each week. The scales don't lie and they will keep you honest. It keeps you on your toes.

MICHELLE SAYS

You need to acknowledge your triggers so you can change old habits. Be aware in the moment that it is happening and you are reverting back to your old behaviour. If you find yourself standing at the fridge, quickly stop and ask, 'What am I doing? What is going on for me?' Maybe you are feeling lonely? You have to register why you are standing in front of the fridge, then change what you are doing immediately.

The contestants have learnt this through painful experience. 'It's so easy to get sucked back into your old life and to slip back into bad habits. If this starts happening, stop and take stock,' advises Munnalita Kyrimis, Season 2. 'One of the best habits I adopted while in the house was keeping a food diary. It made a big difference. Sometimes I would feel like a snack but then I would realise by looking in my diary that I had already consumed close to my kilojoule allocation for that day. If you can write down what you are eating you become aware of your kilojoule intake and it helps a lot.'

'You owe it to yourself to stay on track and remain healthy,' agrees Bryce Harvey, Season 3. 'You have to be tough so you don't slip back into old unhelpful habits. You have to be honest enough to say to yourself, "Mate, you're doing the wrong thing." '

BIGGEST LOSER **BIG** TIP

In the past I'd deal with stressful situations by eating. Since being on the show, my whole focus has changed. Before I'd just feed the cycle by stuffing myself full, then feeling sick, guilty and even more depressed. Now I've discovered I don't have to turn to food. Instead I go outside and get some fresh air, go for a walk or to the gym. It makes me feel a lot better and also clears my mind. That's been a massive change for me.

Kirsten Binnie, Season 3

Practise Persistence!

One thing almost all successful people have in common is the ability to persist. Extraordinary results stem from extraordinary commitment and the determination to push on, no matter what!

Most people who don't achieve their dreams simply give up too early. Don't worry about your past failures. If you see setbacks as momentary glitches and keep pressing on, you will obtain the results you are after. As the proverb goes, 'Failure is the mother of success.'

Trainer Michelle Bridges says, 'Sometimes it's a matter of asking yourself some important questions over and over again. Do I want to eat that, or do I want to feel like this? What are my priorities? Persistence is imperative if you want to stay in the game.'

When faced with adversity, most people quit, but as US President Calvin Coolidge once said: 'Nothing in the world can take the place of persistence. Talent will not; nothing is more common than unsuccessful men with talent. Genius will not; unrewarded genius is almost a proverb. Education will not; the world is filled with educated derelicts. Persistence and determination alone are omnipotent. The slogan "Press on" has solved and always will solve the problems of the human race.'

BIGGEST LOSER BIG TIP

Persistence is everything. Never give up, because the results will come. At times it won't feel like it, but success will happen. Nothing worth striving for in life is easy.

Courtney Jackson, Season 3

Finding the Real Me

Up until *The Biggest Loser* I had always been seen as one half of a set of twins. My entire identity was wrapped up in being half of a duo. Being the youngest, I had unconsciously repressed my personality, relinquished a lot of my power and allowed other people to tell me what to do.

Following the death of my father I used eating as a way to hide from the world, which was just another way of handing over control. I was never an angry person. I simply ate to squash down any uncomfortable feelings before they had time to arise.

In the Biggest Loser house I learnt that I did have my own identity. It was the first time I spent Christmas and my birthday away from my sister and, even though I missed her, I realised I could live my life on my own.

It was a turning point for me – I started to find my own voice and express my feelings. One of the trainers spent a lot of time with me and taught me ways to alter my thinking and deal with my emotions in a more positive way. For instance, when I've had a bad day or am feeling down, rather than turn the negativity inwards, I've learnt to head outside and take the dog for a walk.

Weight loss isn't only about numbers and counting kilojoules. It's how you feel about yourself and giving yourself the life you deserve. I realised it was enough for me to be me and not have to worry about hiding behind a mask or layers of fat.

For the first time in my life I really began to love and enjoy the real me.

Carrianne Rees, Season 3

Handle Setbacks

Although setbacks are a normal part of life and very common when you're trying to lose weight, it's still easy to feel down when you experience a step backwards despite all your hard work and good intentions. But it's not what happens to you but how you deal with it that counts.

When you are faced with failure, treat it as feedback. Take stock of your past attempts, analyse what has worked for you and what hasn't, then apply *The Biggest Loser* winning strategies – including reaching out when you need a hand.

'One of the best ways to stay on track is to recruit all the help you can get,' advocates Carrianne Rees, Season 3. 'You can't always do it alone. I'm a nurse, and people often give us chocolate, so I asked my friends at work to help to keep me accountable. Now I won't even go into the room that the food is in, and people know that if they see me heading that way I need a gentle reminder. Be as strong within yourself as you can, but also ask people to support you. Don't be afraid to ask for help. It doesn't mean you are weak.'

It's also important to view setbacks as temporary, and to have faith. With a little hard work you will move on. Life often comes in waves – you have your good times and those that challenge you, and it's

MICHELLE SAYS

The Biggest Loser lifestyle isn't about getting hot for your wedding or some other short-term goal. This is about forever; it's about being consistent, so if the scales aren't moving, big deal, get over it. Move on. Keep going. They will move eventually. If a slow-moving scale is all that's stopping you, then you have to harden up.

always up to you to choose your response. If you suffer a momentary lapse in progress, what are you going to do? Throw in the towel and turn your back on all your hard work, or persevere until the battle is won?

Many people use a setback as an excuse to avoid hard work or treat it as confirmation that they aren't really meant to succeed. If you find yourself thinking like this, STOP! Remember that EVERY person who has accomplished anything worthwhile has faced what you are going through now. As the old Chinese proverb goes: 'Fall down eight times, get up nine.'

Trainer Shannan Ponton suggests that in times of trouble you focus on your success and recall how far you've come. 'Remember that no-one is perfect. Even Michelle and I both fall off the wagon now and

again. It's just one bad meal, not the end of the earth. But you have to make sure it's just one meal. Don't let it roll over to the next morning. Don't let it snowball. Just address the situation and make up for it. There's no need to beat yourself up. The only time you should be hard with yourself is when you've let yourself go for a few days and you're starting to slip backwards.'

Courtney Jackson, Season 3, admits he put on 7 kilograms shortly after leaving the house. 'One morning I woke up and realised what was happening. I felt terrible, and knew that I was reversing all the hard work I had done. So I got changed into my workout gear and went for an hour-long run. I then continued a high-intensity exercise regime until I had lost the weight. I use fear as a motivating factor because I never want to be the way I was. I refuse to accept my old way of life and that's how I continue to keep the weight off.'

Sometimes the secret to success is simply getting up again and again and again. Kirsten Binnie, Season 3, says, 'Everybody has days where they fall off the wagon, where they don't exercise or they eat chocolate or takeaway and then they feel guilty. The most important thing is to get back on track as soon as possible. So if you have one bad day, don't make it two or three or four bad days. You've had one bad day, so the next day you need to begin again. It's human to fall off the wagon, but the best bit is you can actually turn it around and just get straight back on. It's all about keeping your goals in mind and taking small steps.'

The world is filled with people who have faced setbacks yet have gone on to achieve amazing things. If you experience a slight weight gain or an obstacle in your routine, don't despair. Simply bolster your resolve and carry on!

As you can see, maintaining motivation is easy if you stay positive and refuse to be discouraged. It is disappointing and frustrating when the odds seem stacked against you but it is also good to remember that this is a fabulous opportunity to prove your mettle and shine!

It will help enormously if you follow the wise words of the Biggest Losers and write down your goals. Dedicate part of each day to visualising those goals, persevere with new routines until they become instinctive and practise persistence in the face of setbacks.

BIGGEST LOSER BIG TIP

Persistence and perseverance are the keys to success. If you stick with it, you WILL get there!

Adro Sarnelli, Season 1

Where Are You Now?

If your motiviation is flagging, ask yourself a few hard questions to check if you're on course (in the green zone), drifting a little bit (the orange zone) or heading for the rocks (the red zone). Your aim is to stay in the green zone whenever you can.

GREEN ZONE: Looking Good

If you answer yes to most of these questions you're doing well in the weight-loss game.

☺ You enjoy 3 balanced and satisfying meals and 2 snacks each day.

☺ You always eat a healthy breakfast.

☺ You avoid all white foods, such as white flour, sugar, pasta and rice.

☺ You are conscious of portion size and keep a watch on your overall daily calorie intake.

☺ You drink plenty of water.

☺ You have found a range of exercise techniques that you enjoy and that make you feel good.

☺ You exercise at least 5 days a week, doing cardio, strength, core stability and flexibility workouts.

☺ You keep your appointments for workouts and training sessions.

☺ You incorporate plenty of incidental exercise into your daily routine and strive to be active.

☺ You keep a food and exercise journal to record your food intake, exercise and emotions.

☺ You set realistic targets and work towards them.

☺ You read your goals and visualise your success.

☺ You focus on your strengths and view setbacks as opportunities.

☺ You stay in touch with supportive people who can lend an ear when you're feeling vulnerable.

Real life will sometimes get in the way of your plans and routines. You or a family member may get sick or injured, you may have to travel for an extended time, or move interstate, or take on a big new job, or . . . there will be no end of opportunities for veering off the straight and narrow and into the orange zone. The way to succeed is to expect obstacles to your well-laid plans and not lose heart, but get back on the program as soon as you can. No-one is going to be perfect all the time.

ORANGE ZONE: Watch Out

If you answer yes to most of these questions it's time to ask yourself if you're slipping off track.

- ☺ You can't always be bothered having 3 balanced meals each day.
- ☺ You occasionally skip meals, particularly breakfast.
- ☺ You are snacking more than twice a day and sneaking in more indulgences.
- ☺ You have cravings for sugary, fatty or salty foods and allow yourself refined, white foods.
- ☺ You are drinking less water than before and more caffeinated beverages.
- ☺ You make excuses to avoid the gym or your daily workouts.
- ☺ You haven't exercised for more than three days.
- ☺ You can't lift the same weight for the same number of repetitions as before.
- ☺ Your cardio routine is more taxing and you feel slow and sluggish.
- ☺ You put other responsibilities – like work and household duties – before exercise.
- ☺ You avoid writing in your journal.
- ☺ You make negative comments about yourself.
- ☺ You have stopped thinking about your goals or setting yourself targets.
- ☺ You avoid discussing your progress with people who ask how you're going.

Once you have missed three or four workouts or given yourself permission to deviate from your eating plan a few times it can be all too easy to give in. The greatest temptation is to think, 'Oh well, I've been bad, I may as well keep on being bad.' This is all-or-nothing thinking and this, more than anything, will prevent you from achieving your goals. The most dangerous times are when you have stopped caring. If you find yourself in the red zone, don't give up, but refocus on your hopes and dreams.

RED ZONE: Danger, Danger
If you answer yes to most of these questions, it's time to give yourself a big pep talk and get back on track — pronto!

- ☹ You have stopped planning your meals and snacks.
- ☹ You eat only a couple of servings of fruit and vegetables on most days.
- ☹ You have slipped back into regularly eating refined white foods.
- ☹ You drink alcohol on most days.
- ☹ You eat on the run – in the car, at your desk – and you eat out more often.
- ☹ You get caught up in the moment at social occasions and allow yourself to overindulge.
- ☹ You have not exercised for more than a week.
- ☹ You have decided to take a 'break' from your exercise program for whatever reason.
- ☹ You are less concerned about incidental exercise than before.
- ☹ You have stopped weighing yourself and monitoring your progress.
- ☹ You have stopped keeping a journal.
- ☹ You promise yourself you'll resume your healthy habits eventually and make up for lost time.
- ☹ You don't like to think too far ahead or visualise your health and appearance in the future.
- ☹ You feel angry when someone asks about your progress.

Toughest Moment:
Courtney Jackson, Season 2

When you are losing weight you are challenged physically, emotionally and mentally. All your old habits are just stripped away and you have to confront the person you are underneath. I was an angry person so this meant finding the courage to make myself vulnerable and let that anger slip away. Every aspect of my life changed, but ultimately this was for the better. I am now nothing like the person I used to be.

Best Moment:
Munnalita Kyrimis, Season 2

My best moment came during a trip to New Zealand, when we all had to face our fears. Mine was heights and so I was given a bungee jump to do. I stood on the ledge for 40 minutes, absolutely petrified and unsure if I was able to go ahead with it.

I related the jump to my life in general because I knew it was time to let go. When you jump you release control, and you have nothing to hang on to except faith that things will be okay.

I was literally taking a leap into the unknown.

I finally jumped and it was the best feeling in the world. By taking the leap I felt I was leaving my old habits and life behind. I knew I could face my fears and embrace my future, and it felt fantastic.

6
Staying Fresh

Sticking to a routine can be challenging, particularly if you've been keeping up with all the hard work but your results have started to plateau. In this chapter we look at ways to spice things up when you're feeling lacklustre. *The Biggest Loser* contestants agree that the trick to staying healthy permanently is knowing how to keep things interesting.

Recognise You are in a Rut

While losing weight, a person's weight often stalls at a certain point so the body's organs can adjust. If this happens to you, make some adjustments to your exercise and eating routines and then just keep going.

If you're feeling unmotivated, the first thing to do is admit you are struggling and that it's time to take alternative action.

'Black and white thinking' is dangerous: an 'all or nothing' attitude is not going to serve you well. Try to avoid overreacting to any lull in your progress, and instead focus on keeping up and then varying your routine – no matter what the circumstances, or the mood you find yourself in.

Chipping away at your goal every day always has been and always will be the key to long-term success.

> ## BIGGEST LOSER BIG TIP
>
> Don't make excuses for yourself. I recently injured my knee and in the past I would have used that as an excuse to avoid the gym. These days I might take a little rest but then I am back in there straightaway. Now I keep going, no matter what.
>
> *Garry Guerreiro, Season 3*

Try New Things!

If you are stagnating, simply keep moving! If the monotony of your everyday routine is dragging you down, mix things up and try harder to keep it interesting.

If you have been working out on your own, consider joining forces with an exercise partner. Devise ways you can involve other people in your exercise routine. Is it possible to recruit a work colleague and go power walking or jogging at lunch? Take a training bag to work, pull on your workout gear at lunchtime and take in the local surrounds. This is an excellent way to burn kilojoules and break up your day with some social interaction.

Another great idea is to get away and change your surroundings. Munnalita Kyrimis, Season 2, finds that a short break helps her stay enthusiastic and renews her perspective. 'Sometimes when you get stuck and you aren't seeing the results for your efforts it can bring you down,' she admits. 'When this happens to me I like to go away on a weekend holiday: it energises you and reignites your desire to stay on top.'

Kirsten Binnie, Season 3, agrees. 'From my elite sporting days, I know there are times when you need to stop and have a complete rest. Sometimes your body gets burnt out, and the best thing is to take a

BIGGEST LOSER BIG TIP

I fell into a real rut towards the end of the show where nothing was happening with my weight. I was still working out and watching what I ate and the whole experience was really deflating.

I learnt that a change is as good as a holiday. You've got to vary your routine. I changed my diet and when I ate. I also changed my exercise and took up boxing and went for runs outside rather than just sticking to the treadmill. It made a big difference. After spending weeks at the same weight I suddenly lost 5 kilos.

Garry Guerreiro, Season 3

couple of days off and let yourself recuperate. Allow your body and mind to relax, then start again. Even in the house we gave ourselves a break. Some people on the team were worried that if we stopped we wouldn't lose weight but it worked every time. When we got to the point where we felt burnt out we would stop, take a day off and just relax without doing any training. We'd still watch what we ate but we'd just have fun, muck around and turn the music up loud. It worked really well and always gave us a boost of energy.'

Trainer Michelle Bridges recommends varying your routine. 'I like to change the route I run on,' she says. 'If I get bored, I'll drive myself to the beach and do a run there. I go and try new things I haven't done before. I'll jump in on a boxing class or do some kickboxing. When my husband and I go away on a holiday we hire bikes and ride around the whole time. It keeps it fresh and interesting.'

Consider taking up a new sport or hobby. You only live once, so why not just go for it! Some exciting activities to try include:

- Indoor rockclimbing
- Ballroom dancing
- Dragon boat racing
- Indoor soccer
- Swimming at the local pool
- Joining a cricket team
- Mountain bike riding
- Martial arts such as kung-fu and taekwondo
- Whitewater rafting
- Kayaking
- Playing tennis
- Sailing

Alison Braun, Season 3, says, 'Since being on *The Biggest Loser* I have learnt to try new things. The other week I decided to go rockclimbing for the first time and loved it! I would never have tried anything like that before. I asked a few of the people close to me if they would come but everyone was busy so I ended up going by myself and had a ball! I went again shortly after and it was great to see my teenage son looking up at me saying, "My mum can get up the side of a rock faster than I can!" '

It's true we gravitate towards what brings us joy in life, so the best way to stay motivated with your exercise regimen is to make it fun. Now is the time to be creative and devise new ways for keeping up your energy and momentum.

Dull habits can rob you of the invigorating life you deserve, so if you feel your enthusiasm waning, do something new and enjoyable to help you feel revitalised. Get up early and go for a walk, climb a mountain and watch the sun set, or dive into the ocean for an invigorating swim. Use your imagination and seek out the excitement in life.

Kirsten Binnie, Season 3, found that her weight loss plateaued for a few weeks towards the end of the series. The solution, she found, was variety. 'Your body becomes accustomed to a certain program so if you are doing the same thing every week with your food and exercise your body just gets used to it and doesn't burn fat as efficiently. Mixing it up is the key. Try a different aerobics class, do some boxing or perhaps swap trainers for a week or two. Do something different to shock your body into realising it still has work to do.'

Keep Your Eating in Check

If you have hit a plateau, now is also the time to review your eating habits and cut down on kilojoules. 'Unconscious eating' – that is, not realising you are consuming as much as you are – can really set you back. The best way to handle this is to record every morsel that passes your lips and ensure you are burning an adequate number of kilojoules through physical activity.

Analyse every aspect of your daily eating plan – are your portion sizes getting bigger? Are you adding sauces and condiments? Have you been dining out, or loading up on excess carbs?

If you find yourself eating for reasons other than hunger, ask yourself what the problem is, then take the appropriate action to get back on track.

Munnalita Kyrimis, Season 2, advocates sticking to a food plan. 'My major plan of attack is not to have junk food in the first place,' she says. 'Because I am an

emotional eater it is better not to store any junk food in the house. I buy food when I need it rather than keep it in the cupboard. When I eat alone I keep it very simple and basic so I'm not tempted to overeat and I always stick to a food plan of three meals and two healthy snacks a day.

'For breakfast I usually have a small bowl of cereal such as oats with skinny milk and some fruit, or a yoghurt, and I make sure I eat breakfast every day without fail. I know that if I skip breakfast I will have cravings mid-morning and feel tempted to resort to junk food. For lunch and dinner I have grilled fish, chicken or meat with grilled or boiled vegies, and for snacks I like a handful of almonds, some yoghurt or a piece of fruit. If I'm going to have bread I stick to no more than 2 slices a day and I have it at lunch rather than dinner.

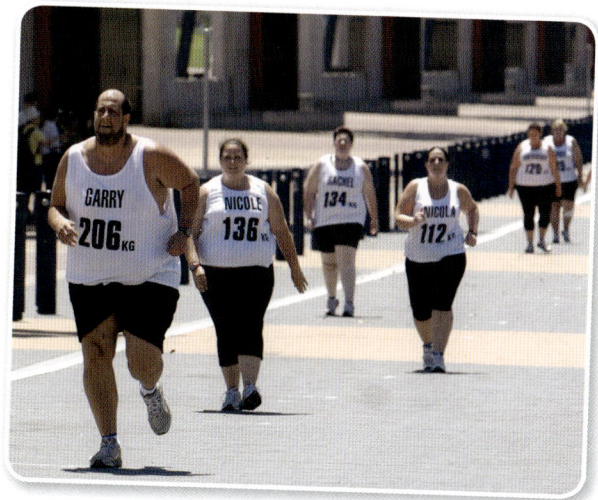

'Most importantly, if I have an event coming up where I'm likely to eat a few treats, I do some extra exercise that week, or cut back my food intake on other days. It means constant monitoring – sometimes I feel like I have a weight-loss channel playing in my head. I'm a lot more conscious now and am always aware of the food I consume. I know that if I eat a bit extra then I have to make up for it so I won't put on weight.'

Another reason for a sudden kilojoule creep could be that you are bored with your daily eating regimen. If this is the case, it's time to invest in some healthy eating cookbooks and try new recipes.

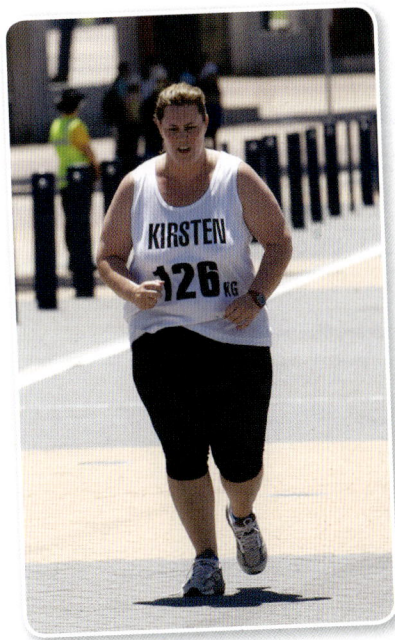

Get Enough Sleep

Getting a good night's sleep is essential to long-term health and helps prevent disruption of the hormones that control appetite. Some research even links a lack of sleep to being overweight. In a study published by the Archives of Internal Medicine, it was documented that overweight and obese men and women tended to sleep for a shorter period of time each night than those with a normal body mass index.

This is because sleep loss affects the levels of leptin, the hormone that controls appetite, telling you when you have had enough to eat. Leptin is released by fat cells in the body and works simultaneously with ghrelin, the hormone that increases appetite and is released by the stomach to stimulate hunger. When leptin levels are lowered or ghrelin levels are increased, ghrelin becomes the dominant hormone, sending a signal to the brain that you are hungry and encouraging you to eat.

The study concluded that an additional 20 minutes of sleep each night may be all that is needed to help lower your body mass index.

The effects of a good night's sleep also include a stronger immune system, better concentration, greater emotional stability and mental resources, and improved mood – all further incentives to get some extra shut-eye.

Although many people claim they don't exercise because they are too tired, working out can actually help you sleep better, and thus give you more energy to do more exercise the next day. It's a win-win situation! One study showed that adults who engaged in moderate exercise 4 times a week for approximately half an hour to an hour per session slept better than those who remained inactive.

Pati Singe, Season 2, found losing weight greatly improved her sleep. 'One of the first things we did when we went into the house was a sleep test. The results showed that I was suffering from sleep apnoea, which is where you actually stop breathing in your sleep. It's quite common among people who are overweight. A few months later I did another test and did a lot better! Losing weight meant that I was sleeping better and breathing better.'

According to the Victorian Department of Health, the average adult should aim for eight hours' sleep each night, although each individual should be guided by their own levels of alertness. If you feel drowsy during the day, that is your body's way of telling you to sleep more.

BIGGEST LOSER BIG TIP

Not getting enough sleep really affects your moods and can also trigger cravings for carbohydrates. I'm a nurse, which means lots of night shifts and you don't always get the sleep you need. Some days you have to be at work really early and at other times you work through the night, so your body clock is all over the place. Lack of sleep does bring on my cravings for carbs but I stick to my rule – no carbohydrates after lunchtime! If I feel like something sweet after lunch, I grab an apple and have a big drink of water or some diet soft drink.

Carrianne Rees, Season 3

Be Responsible

One of the most powerful things you can do is to become the orchestrator of your own dreams. Refuse to let external forces hold you back from reaching your goals. Accept that if you want to lose weight and keep it off, the responsibility is yours, and yours alone.

Courtney Jackson, Season 2, agrees. 'How badly do you want this?' he asks. 'Would you rather go to the gym for 30 minutes for a workout or sit on the couch feeling lethargic and miserable? The choice is always yours and what you do with your life is entirely up to you. No-one can do the work for you. If you are tired, then move it. You will always feel better after a workout.'

If your progress feels slow, you have to find ways to break through until you succeed. Recognising that you are in control of your body and your actions allows you to take charge of your life and destiny.

Garry Guerreiro, Season 3, says, 'To take control of your destiny you need to be responsible. If you just sit on your couch and watch TV, you are not going to achieve much. I always appeared to be a pretty happy-go-lucky guy, but in reality it was a cover. Being overweight does play on your mind. You can make a decision to sit around and be unhappy for the next ten years, or do something about it. Now I've lost 70 kilograms I feel fantastic. If you want to be happy and successful in life, you need to look after yourself: it's as simple as that.'

If you have tried to lose weight before, you will know how easy it is to lose heart when the results level out. You are working hard but with little to show for it. It's frustrating and you may consider giving in. At this point it is extremely important that you don't make excuses for yourself and blame external forces. Changing your ways and taking responsibility for your weight and life can be difficult, but ultimately it is one of the most rewarding things you can do.

Vitality and vigour come from a sense of purpose, so when you do what excites you it propels you even further towards your dream. Know what you want, vow you are worth it, take responsibility for owning and living your best life and enjoy the rewards.

Adro Sarnelli, Season 1, reveals he was almost ready to quit when the scales refused to budge. 'I had steadily lost small amounts of weight and then the scales almost stopped moving altogether. By the fourth week I told the trainers I was going to leave the show. Then trainer Bob came and took me under his wing – he cared for me, spoke to me and showed me new ways of dieting and attacking my training. The very next week I dropped 7.7 kilograms, which was amazing. I'm so glad I didn't give in and throw it all away. I learnt a valuable lesson: we have to keep trying new things until we find the solution.'

Keep up the Momentum

You reap what you sow. If you are committed to sowing the 'good' seeds day in and day out, you will eventually reap your harvest. Input determines your results, so keep up the hard work and have faith that you will eventually see the benefit of your efforts.

As your commitment strengthens, you will build momentum that can keep you going even on tough days. Momentum helps you maintain your enthusiasm and passion, and allows your new way of living to become habitual. The best thing you can do when faced with a lull is to push through and be confident that success will come.

If you lose momentum, though, it's useful to consider why. Is there a reason your productivity and effectiveness have stalled? Now that you are eradicating the layers, are you comfortable with the 'real' you being exposed? Are you procrastinating? Is a fear of success holding you back?

Fear will stop you in your tracks and paralyse you, but only if you let it. Courage is acting not in the absence of fear, but in spite of fear, so be brave and keep moving onwards, whether you feel like it or not! Make sure you do not procrastinate or make excuses to stay where you are. Move on from your comfort zone.

To gain in life, we must take risks and that means moving and building momentum. It takes time, courage and commitment to leave the armour behind and live a life of truth. 'Leap and the net will appear' is a great mantra to live by and encourages you to be brave and risk leaving your old, limiting life in the past.

BIGGEST LOSER BIG TIP

Garry's 'Company of Life' Epiphany

I realised one day that weight loss is like maintaining a job. If you want to get far you need to put in the work and effort.

If you want to be fat, sit back, dial a pizza and eat takeaway. It's no effort. But if you want to be healthy, live longer and enjoy a greater quality of life then, like progressing at work, you have to put in the extra hours.

Life is just like one big company. If you want to get somewhere you've got to show you're ambitious and put in the hard yards.

Garry Guerreiro, Season 3

SHANNAN'S TOP TIPS FOR STAYING FRESH

1 Variety

It's important that you regularly change the way you train. If you've been walking, challenge yourself to start running, or try out a spin, aerobics or circuit class. Varying the style of training will help you stay motivated and excited.

2 Join a team

Become part of a netball, basketball, football or soccer team. Or perhaps you might want to consider joining a fun run team that trains on the weekend, and set yourself the goal of running in a City to Surf or other form of marathon. Joining forces with other people keeps you accountable.

3 Set yourself a goal or challenge

Introducing a competitive element to your training makes things interesting and gives you something to aim for.

Results always come, so if you find yourself lagging or lacking in motivation don't despair. By recognising that you have stagnated you can take positive action. Keep things fresh and interesting by revisiting your existing exercise regimen and eating plan and mixing things up a bit. Ensure you get enough sleep and take responsibility for your health and life choices. Stick with the program, build momentum and go forward with a heart of faith.

With a little imagination, lots of action and a dash of good old-fashioned bravado, you will find yourself in the land of success before you know it.

Toughest Moment:
Alison Braun, Season 3

My toughest moment was being away from my family at Christmas, missing my children's birthdays and my youngest daughter's first day of school. Up until that time I had always been there for my family and they had always been my top priority. It was a difficult thing to get my head around because I felt selfish for putting myself first.

PATI

ORIGINAL WEIGHT

120.2

CURRENT WEIGHT

72.2

DIFFERENCE

-48.0

LG

Best Moment:
Pati Singe, Season 2

My best moment was in New Zealand, when we were given a triathlon challenge that involved bike riding, canoeing and kayaking. I was up against two boys and someone in the group said, 'We know who will win – it will be both the boys.' Something in me just clicked and I thought, 'We'll see about that!' I refused to give in to the odds and decided to give it my absolute best. It was the first time I can ever remember just giving it my all and refusing to hold back.

I really surprised myself. I put every ounce of my being into that challenge and I ended up giving the boys a really good race. We were neck and neck all the way.

It was a pivotal moment in my life because I beat my fear of failure. In the past I had always made excuses for myself, whereas in this instant I completely relinquished my safety net. I had nothing to fall back on and it felt exhilarating. It was such an accomplishment, realising my full potential. I thought, 'It's amazing what I can do when I put my mind to it!'

From that day on I have allowed myself to invest in things more. Now I work really hard towards achieving the targets I set for myself.

7

Surviving in the Real World: Facing Everyday Situations

If you've been following the advice of the Biggest Losers, you are now exercising regularly, eating three balanced meals a day, visualising your success and keeping a diary or food journal.

Like most people who are losing weight, you have probably encountered everyday situations in which you feel tempted to break with your program. Maybe it has been at a work event, during a lazy holiday away or dining out at a restaurant for a friend's birthday.

Surviving everyday temptations takes planning and preparation. You will often be confronted with unhealthy food and feel the pressure or need to consume it. It will take strength, willpower and discipline to rise above the occasion and exercise your right to say 'no'.

In this chapter, *The Biggest Loser* contestants reveal their sure-fire ways for staying fantastically fit and healthy, even after they left the show and were faced with all the real-world temptations of daily living.

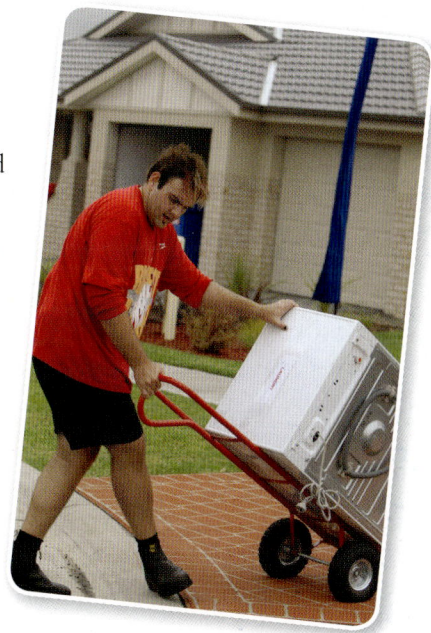

Prioritise Your Health

The great German writer Goethe said, 'Things which matter most should never be at the mercy of those which matter least.' This is a great reminder to assess your priorities in life. Do your everyday actions reflect what is important to you?

Your actions must support your overall objective of staying in shape, and your daily decisions should make it clear that you value your wellbeing above anything else.

Sometimes this means standing out and not conforming to the crowd. For example, if all your workmates socialise on a Friday afternoon and pizza and beer are the only food and drink options, you will have to decide to put your health before your desire to fit in, and refrain from eating and drinking like everyone else.

Living a healthy life means being serious about making and keeping commitments to yourself. It means honouring your path and ensuring you stand strong, even in the face of temptation. Accept that

It helps to keep your goals in mind at all times. When I was in the house I posted up photos around my bed of all the people I wanted to impress when I got out of the house. Every day I would look at the photos and imagine their faces when they saw the new me. I knew that my dad would be so happy to see me lose weight and so I focused on that. When I couldn't do it for myself I thought about the people I cared about and how much they wanted to see me achieve my goals.

Garry Guerreiro, Season 3

there will be times when it's hard to say 'no' and walk away, but also acknowledge the gratification you feel when you respect yourself enough to put your own needs first.

Once you know what your priorities are in life, it becomes easier to pay attention to those things that truly matter. Being a healthy and vital individual will benefit everything else you do – from your work productivity and relationships to living your dreams – and when you truly understand this, refraining from that after-work fatty 'treat' becomes a cinch!

Trainer Shannan Ponton emphasises the importance of being selective when dining out. 'You always have the choice of eating healthily,' he says. 'Every restaurant will do a chicken breast or lean piece of steak with some vegies or salad. If it's not on the menu it doesn't mean you can't ask for it. It's a matter of being disciplined and making sure you get the grilled fish with salad rather than the battered fish with chips.'

'Coming off the show and going back to everyday situations was definitely challenging,' confesses Kirsten Binnie, Season 3. 'If you are faced with certain temptations, such as chocolate, you just have to have a couple of pieces rather than the whole block. It's about moderation. If you feel like a Mars Bar, eat a snack size one instead of a full-sized one, or if you know you'll be going out for dinner and eating a bit more than usual, make sure you fit in some extra exercise that day. If I go out at night, I get up early and go for a run so it will make up for what I will be eating later on.'

The Importance of Planning

Remember that spectacular achievements are always preceded by painstaking preparation and it's important to plan whenever you can. Research shows that people eat more when they are in a group than when alone, so it's important you are prepared when dining with others.

If eating out at a restaurant, make sure you don't arrive ravenous! By fasting for hours before your outing you actually propel your body into 'starvation mode', and may feel tempted to dive into the breadbasket on arrival. One idea is to eat a couple of spoonfuls of low-fat natural yoghurt with a handful of almonds mid-afternoon to keep hunger pangs at bay so you arrive at the restaurant feeling in control.

At this stage of the game, you may also want to exercise some flexibility with your eating. For instance, if you know that you have a special occasion

MICHELLE SAYS

Stay organised. If you know you're going out for dinner, make sure you don't arrive starving. Grab a snack before you go – something healthy like a piece of fruit or a few rice crackers with cottage cheese. When you get to the restaurant, order two entrees rather than an entree and a main. And make smart choices. When I go out I have the grilled fish and salad rather than the veal parmigiana with all the cheese and slop on top. If you can steer the direction of where you eat that can help enormously too. Rather than ending up at an Indian place, suggest you go for Thai – that way you can order a really nice Thai beef salad.

BIGGEST LOSER BIG TIP

A fantastic idea is to substitute a frozen yoghurt for dessert. I put a low-fat strawberry yoghurt in the freezer and have it instead of ice-cream. It tastes great!

Munnalita Kyrimis, Season 2

coming up, you may cut back on your snacks for that week or take your exercise routine up a notch so you can enjoy dessert on the night. Balance is the key, however, and it is important that if you eat dessert one night, it doesn't become a habit. Remember, a habits is anything you do *repeatedly* – so if you are exercising and eating healthily most of the time, the odd dessert is okay.

Another great way to stay in control is by taking a packed lunch to work. Invest in a lunch box and fill it up with a colourful salad, a couple of low-fat crispbreads or slices of wholegrain bread, a small tin of tuna and a piece of fruit. Not only will you save money, but you'll also have a healthy lunch, rather than relying on your work cafeteria.

Kirsten Binnie, Season 3, cooks extra portions at dinnertime and packs a healthy homemade meal for work the next day. 'I always vary my lunches. Usually I have some rice or pasta and vegetables, or a sandwich. I also like low-fat soup in winter, with a crusty bread roll, which is really tasty and a great way to fill you up. I generally have my carbs at lunch and just have meat and vegetables for dinner.'

When visiting the supermarket always take a list, and never go grocery shopping when you are hungry – it will only encourage you to fill up your trolley with high-fat, high-kilojoule 'treats'.

It is also a great idea to keep a gym bag handy at work so you can go power walking or jogging at lunch. Or keep a skipping rope at home, turn up the music and skip to your favourite song whenever you feel a craving coming on.

Ask yourself how you can be optimally healthy at any given point throughout the day.

Avoid Temptations

Everyday temptations can strike in many forms, and it's up to you to identify what they are and how you will avoid them. When they left the Biggest Loser house, all the contestants had to face temptation and learn how to maintain their healthy habits in the real world.

Whether it's dining out at a restaurant, socialising or even chilling out at home, there will always be the lure of everyday treats to tempt you. Try to pause before you eat – ask yourself if you are eating for emotional reasons, or to fit in socially. A useful strategy is to step aside, take a few deep breaths, and grab a glass of refreshing iced water instead.

Unlike other addictions such as alcohol or cigarettes, it is impossible to go 'cold turkey' with food. After all, it is essential to life. Moreover, food plays a significant role in every culture. It is celebration, religion, national identity, ritual and more. So, sooner or later you are going to find yourself in a situation in which food is central to the occasion, such as a birthday party, Christmas lunch at your mother-in-law's, an office function or a barbecue at your mate's new house . . . the sorts of occasions when it would be rude not to participate. You just need to be prepared.

'So much of our social and cultural activity revolves around eating,' says Munnalita, Season 2. 'It is a custom that people meet up and eat. Now I have ways of ensuring that I can still socialise without putting on weight. Often I just order an entree instead of a main course and if I feel like dessert I go halves with my husband.

'I really watch my portion control. Your eyes are bigger than your belly so you have to be aware of how much you eat. I'm very conscious of what I eat now and know that I have to stop before I'm full. Before *The Biggest Loser* I would eat even after I felt full because I liked the taste. Now I realise it's just not worth it.

'Sometimes if I know the food on offer won't be particularly healthy I eat before I go out and just meet people for a drink. It's all about planning and being prepared.'

It's a good idea to remind yourself that food is not the only reason for the gathering. It's about spending time with people and enjoying their company. Focus on your companions and relish the moment. Not everything has to be about food and what you eat.

EATING OUT WITHOUT **BLOWING** OUT

▶ Don't use a special event as an excuse to blow your healthy eating plan – moderation and balance still count. But if you do eat more than usual, don't allow your enjoyment of the outing to put a dent in your self-esteem.

▶ Eating a handful of walnuts, a small bowl of sugar-free yoghurt or a cup of low-calorie soup before you go out will help to take the edge off your appetite.

▶ You are likely to be served much larger portions than usual in a restaurant. You could order a salad instead of an entree and then an entree instead of a main meal.

▶ Drink a glass of water before your meal arrives. And keep your hands off that bread roll.

▶ Ask for vegetables or a salad instead of chips, pasta or rice.

▶ Beware of creamy sauces and high-fat dressings. They can add a whole load of unwanted extra calories to food that would otherwise be healthy.

▶ Watch how much you drink. Not only is alcohol full of 'empty' kilojoules, it also loosens inhibitions and destroys self-discipline so you're more likely to eat more than you intended. Pace yourself and stay hydrated by drinking plenty of water.

▶ When it comes to dessert, share with someone else, or stick to something light like fruit or sorbet.

▶ If you're the kind of person who really likes to get stuck in at a social gathering it might help to pace yourself against the slowest eater or drinker. Try to be the last to start eating and eat and drink slowly.

▶ Remember, you don't have to eat everything on your plate.

Temptation can also strike when you are at home, perhaps when you are relaxing in front of the television. Sometimes the mere mention of a high-sugar treat in an ad break can be enough to spark a craving. The best way to avoid this situation is to:

1   Mute the volume on the TV during ads and turn your attention to other things – engage in a conversation with the person next to you, paint your nails or tackle something on your 'to do' list. Fill in those minutes by doing something productive.

2   Use the ad breaks to get your metabolism going. Hit the floor and do some sit-ups or grab your skipping rope and do some jumps. Make sure that 'ad time' equals 'exercise time' and soon your TV viewing will be an entirely new experience.

If you are responsible for meal preparation for the rest of the family, be careful. It is easy to nibble while cooking, or to consume leftovers when clearing the dishes. Promise yourself that you will only ever eat when sitting down at the table. This will alleviate the problem of unconsciously consuming excess kilojoules while doing something else.

This also applies to eating in your car. Remember, it doesn't matter where you consume the food: it still counts! If you stop to fill your car up with petrol, resist reaching for the snack bar at the counter. If you feel like a treat, purchase a non-food item such as a magazine or CD to listen to as you drive. Vow to resist the 'drive thru' at fast-food outlets at all costs.

Garry Guerreiro, Season 3, advocates enjoying all things in moderation. 'I view eating a bit like drink driving – you can only have so much otherwise you go over the limit. I know I can only have so many treats per week and then I've reached my limit. If I have a piece of cake I make sure it is only a small piece and I do a little extra in my workout the next day. On the show we were extremely controlled in what we ate and for the majority of the time I am still quite vigilant. However, I now allow myself to enjoy the odd treat, as long as I don't overdo it.'

It's important to obtain your happiness from sources other than food. Any sense of satisfaction you experience from overindulging is only momentary and will give way to lasting feelings of regret.

Alison Braun, Season 3, reveals since leaving the house she has swapped chocolate for exercise. 'Exercise is now my stress release. It's my "me time". I find training quite therapeutic. I just zone out and train hard, and it feels fantastic at the end of the session when I know I've done something healthy and positive for myself.'

Good food and healthy options are always out there – it's up to you to prioritise your health every day, and at every occasion. Remember to revisit your goals, keep visualising and stay focused whether you are at a restaurant, a party, relaxing at home or driving in your car. You are in control and have the ability to make empowering decisions wherever you are.

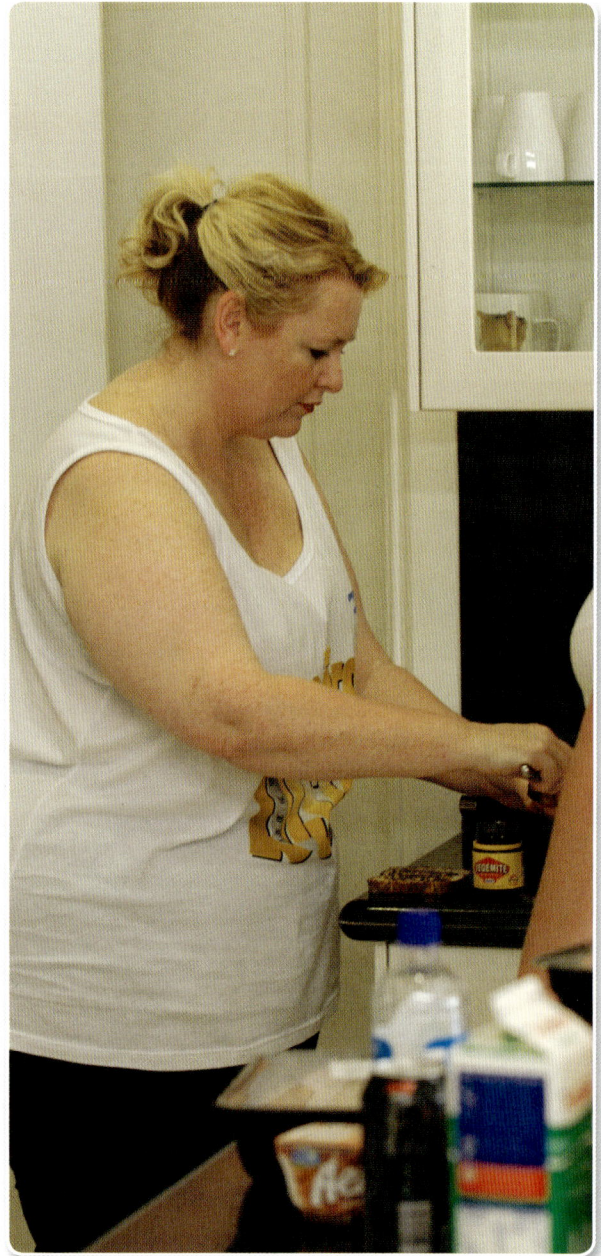

BIGGEST LOSER BIG TIP

It is vital you extend yourself past your comfort zone if you want to be successful. If you look at anyone successful in life they are the ones who have been persistent and consistent, followed their dreams and kept working at it.

Alison Braun, Season 3

Extend Yourself

Success comes down to being willing to do what the average person is not willing to do – that is, pushing yourself beyond your normal capabilities and taking yourself out of your comfort zone.

In many martial arts, such as kung-fu, students are encouraged to push their bodies physically, to reach and stretch themselves as far as they can go. At times this can be painful, but it's all about making the most of what you've been given. Apply this principle to everyday life and treat every outing, social situation and temptation as an opportunity to grow, strengthen and develop yourself. Just like a student of kung-fu, you can become the master of your body and mind.

BIGGEST LOSER BIG TIP

Being healthy is a constant effort. Focus on how far you have come and remind yourself of the advantages of healthy living.

Pati Singe, Season 2

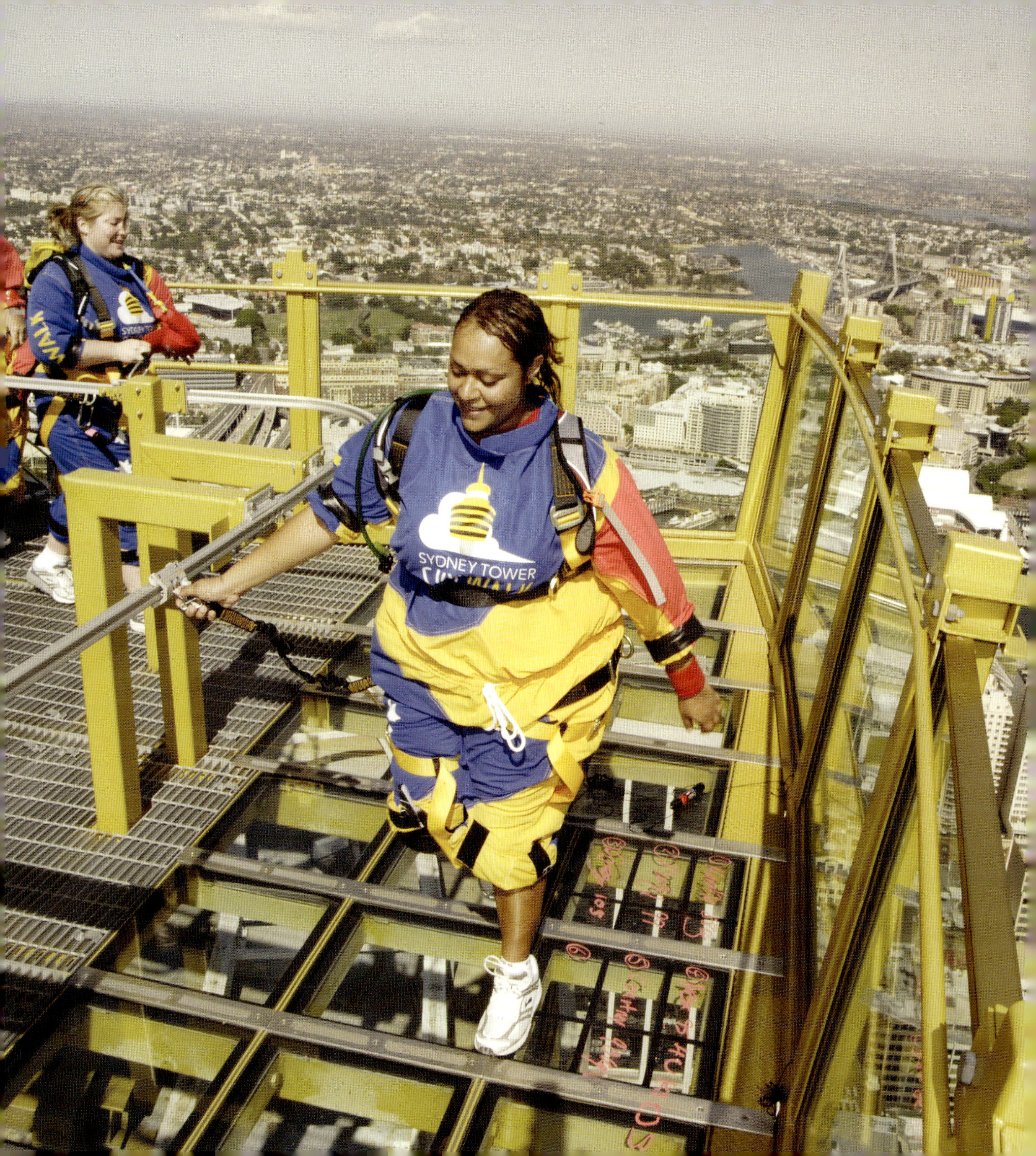
SYDNEY TOWER

Choose Healthy Relationships

All the Biggest Losers realise the importance of surrounding yourself with positive and supportive people. You are ultimately responsible for your weight loss, but having a group of supportive people on hand is invaluable for those times when you feel vulnerable.

Sadly, those closest to you can sometimes be the ones who most resist seeing you change. Perhaps subconsciously they fear that you will become a different person and there won't be room in your new life for them any more. Maybe they are suddenly forced to confront their own issues with weight, or now have trouble expressing their love if your relationship was previously based on their 'gift' of food.

Generally, the source of their unease is fear. Fortunately, there is something you can do about this – involve them! Let the people close to you know how much you appreciate their support and give them practical ways they can assist you. Ask them to join you by going for walks together, taking a healthy cooking class or joining a club and starting up a new hobby. Encourage and motivate them to be a part of your healthy life.

Trainer Shannan Ponton warns: 'Saboteurs are everywhere. The best way to deal with them is to invite them to join you on your journey and to share in the benefits of being fit and healthy. Say "Come to

the gym with me. Let's add another hour together in our day where we can share the same experience." '

Alison Braun, Season 3, admits, 'After I lost the weight certain people would try to feed me up. They would comment that I was looking too thin, when in reality I was looking and feeling great. I understand that it comes from a place of fear, but it's up to them to deal with the changes that have taken place. I try to have as much empathy as possible, as I know it can be hard for people to accept change. I let them know how much I value their support while continuing to stay strong within myself.'

If a particular friend or family member is still resistant, the best thing to do is sit down and have an honest talk with them about how you value the relationship and want to see it grow. Let them know you are serious about your lifestyle choices and have made an ongoing commitment to change. If they continue to be unsupportive, perhaps it's time to establish some boundaries and protect yourself.

Courtney Jackson, Season 2, explains, 'Sometimes people are unsure of the new person emerging from the layers. I had people in my life who struggled with the fact I had become more confident, independent and self-assured, and even though I was happier, they didn't want to embrace the new me. Everyone will have these sorts of people in their lives. Maybe it is a jealous friend who is now more overweight than you and the dynamic of the friendship has changed.

'Perhaps it's a partner who is scared that you will now attract more attention from the opposite sex. If you are struggling with your weight, the last thing you need is people trying to drag you down. I felt that if people weren't willing to embrace the new happier and healthier me, they weren't really my friends. In the end, perhaps it's best to distance yourself from

those people who don't want to see you happy and strong. I choose my friends very carefully now – they are always people who want the best for me.'

Of course, many of your relationships will improve as a result of your new healthy lifestyle. Adro Sarnelli, Season 1, says, 'My relationship with my daughter changed in a really big way. I could finally be the father I had always wanted to be; the kind that could get up and run with my kids in the park. The first time I went to an indoor play centre after I appeared on *The Biggest Loser*, my daughter Odessa asked me to come in and play with her. I started to say, "Sorry, but Daddy can't fit," just like all the other times before, but then I realised I could! So I went in and played with her and after an hour and a half she asked if we could go home because she was tired. It was the best feeling. Finally I was free from being overweight!'

Always remember, though – whether or not you have those closest to you on board, YOU are ultimately responsible for your own wellbeing.

BIGGEST LOSER BIG TIP

If you want to be successful, it is crucial you surround yourself with positive and supportive people. You need people who are there to help you and who want to see you succeed. You want to surround yourself with people who will stop you falling and help you fly.

Adro Sarnelli, Season 1

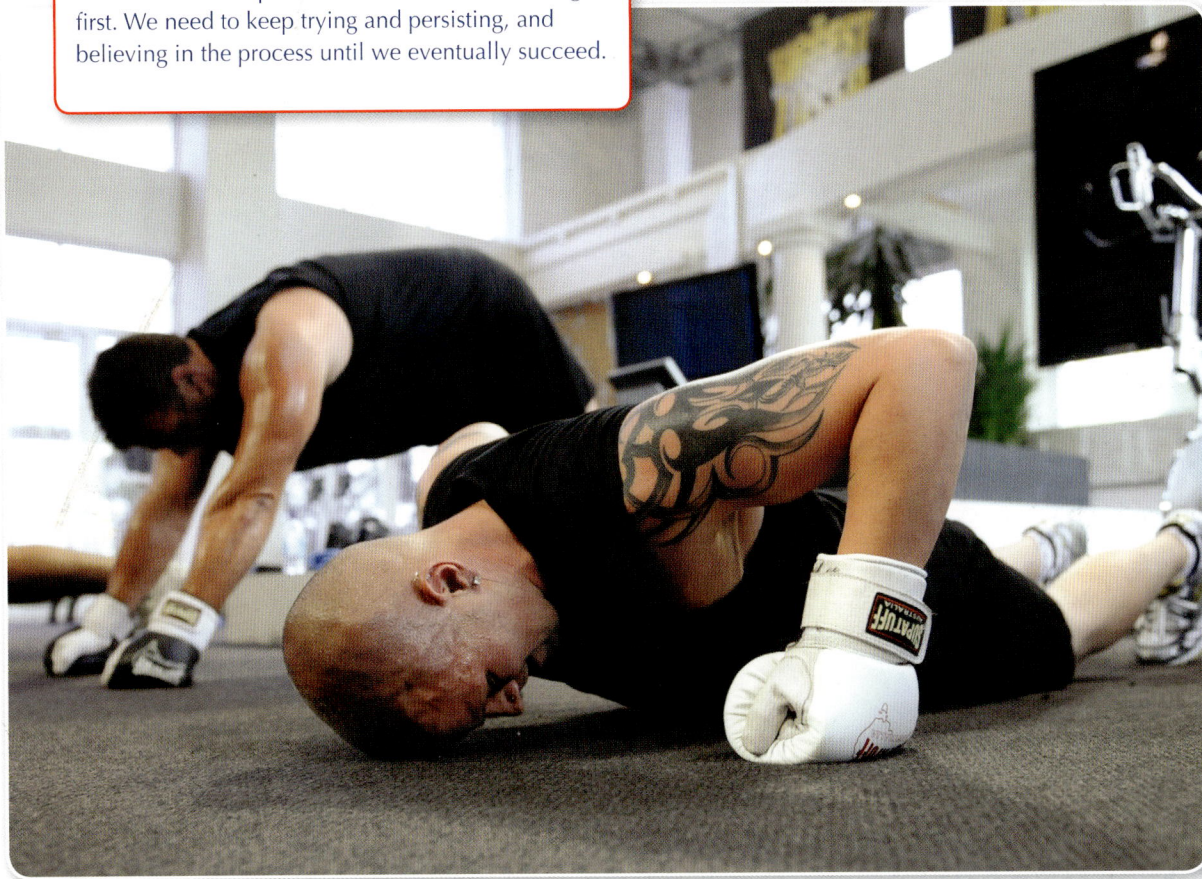

Best Moment:
Bryce Harvey, Season 3

My best moment was winning a challenge in the sand dunes. I had been kicked out of the house but when I won the race it gave me the opportunity to go back on the show.

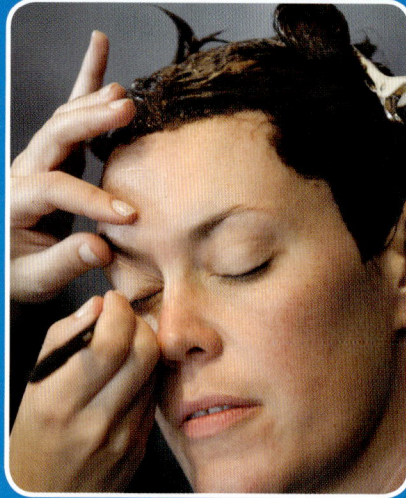

8
Post-Loser Living: The New Healthy You!

Throughout this book you have discovered the secret success strategies behind the Biggest Losers' incredible life-changing experiences.

You have been privy to the internal struggles the contestants have faced, but also the incredible results they enjoyed at the end of all their hard work. You will have realised that *The Biggest Loser* philosophy isn't just a quick fix diet – it's a guide for life.

The Biggest Losers all acknowledge their time in the house was a gift that enabled them to lose weight and change their lives, but they also realise that maintaining their new-found way of living requires regular effort. In this chapter we look at how the Biggest Losers have kept their weight off after leaving the house, the practical and psychological techniques they employ and how they continue to thrive.

Maintenance is an Attitude – for Life!

Studies have shown that less than one quarter of all people who lose weight keep it off for more than two years. But since appearing on the show many Biggest Losers have maintained their weight loss. So what gives them the winning edge?

Munnalita Kyrimis, Season 2, reveals it takes 'constant effort'. 'I am conscious of everything I eat and what I put into my body and how much I need to exercise. Since coming off the show I have realised how lost I was before – it was like I was living in a haze. I finally feel like I am on top of things.'

It is going to take focus and vigilance to maintain your new healthy body and mind by refusing to turn to food in times of trouble and making time for exercise, but by adhering to the steps outlined in the previous chapters you can definitely do it!

As Courtney Jackson, Season 2, notes, it takes commitment to maintain your weight. 'If you stop eating healthily and don't exercise, your weight will balloon. Weight loss boils down to diligence and time.

'You know what needs to be done to achieve the results you want. If you apply what you have learnt, you will be able to maintain your ideal weight. I exercise for 45 minutes, five days a week. It's not a chore – it's because I enjoy it. Diets don't work. A long-term lifestyle change is the only way. I've gone on countless diets throughout my life and have always bounced back to my original weight, and even put more on. I finally feel like I am in control and it's because I commit myself to healthy living every single day.'

Trainer Shannan Ponton says, 'The body does not magically reset itself – life won't suddenly become easier when you lose weight. You have to maintain your healthy eating and exercise plan and make sure that your calories in equal your calories out, otherwise you will put the weight back on. You are going to have good days and you are going to have bad days. The main thing is you have to stop when you slip up, address the problem, then take the weight back off again.'

BIGGEST LOSER BIG TIP

It feels great to go out for dinner and for the emphasis to be on the social aspect rather than the food. It is empowering to sit there and only eat what you need and to feel in control. I'm into small portions now – I often order something like an antipasto plate and pick at that. I pay more attention to the people I'm with rather than overeating like I used to. People take notice and I think it inspires others to become healthier too.

Munnalita Kyrimis, Season 2

For Garry Guerreiro, Season 3, *The Biggest Loser* has permanently changed his outlook. 'Weight loss is not just about eating the right things and exercising, it's a completely new way of thinking. You have to take control of your life and allow your new way of being to become habitual. It's important to keep your thinking in check and be doing all the right things so the weight doesn't come flying back on.'

As Helen Keller said: 'When we do the best we can, we never know what miracle will come into our life, or the life of another.' By remaining dedicated to your dream you will not only attract great things into your own life but you will also undoubtedly inspire others.

Carrianne Rees, Season 3, agrees: 'A lot of the nurses at work now ask me to train them and help them lose weight. I take a salad to work for lunch and so a few others do the same now. I've also managed to get a few of my close friends to the gym so we all go and work out together. It's so much better when you have friends to keep you motivated.'

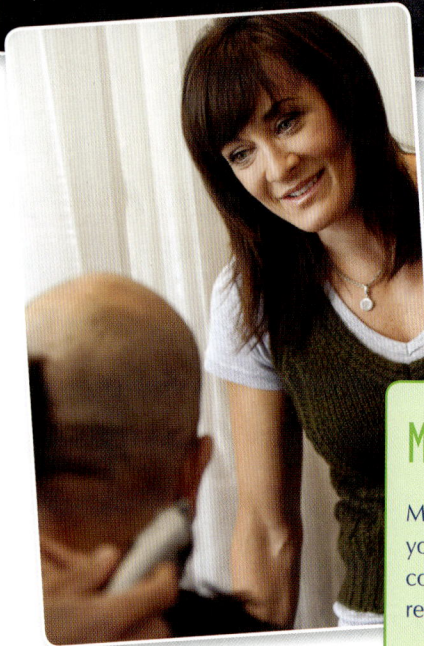

MICHELLE SAYS

Maintaining your health is a daily event. Every day you have to choose well. It always comes back to consistency. You have to make the smart choices in regards to exercise and nutrition every single day.

Protect Your Health

When you enjoy great health, everything else in life becomes easier – you have more vitality, a greater degree of confidence and higher levels of energy. When you have something of value, you need to treasure, protect and nurture it. Your health will always be your greatest asset, so you have to guard it vigorously.

Take practical measures to ensure that nothing gets in the way of you living the best life you can imagine. This could be as simple as remaining flexible and varying your day-to-day routine – tackling the gym instead of going for an outside run if it's raining, packing your lunch for work every day so you are not at the mercy of the cafeteria, or becoming more assertive with friends and requesting to meet up for a walk instead of going to a cafe for cake.

BIGGEST LOSER BIG TIP

There are going to be times when you eat the wrong things or don't do enough exercise. If that happens you have to nip it in the bud before it becomes an issue. I've gone up in weight and I've made myself come back down – that's normal. No-one is perfect but as long as you keep plugging away you are on the road to a happy and enjoyable life.

Bryce Harvey, Season 3

Watch your moods and thoughts, and monitor your mental health carefully. Are there certain times when you tend to revert back to your old unhelpful ways of thinking? Your physical health is a representation of your inner state of being, so be sure to practise cognitive behaviour techniques regularly. It is vital that you deal with any negative emotions such as anger, fear and frustration as they arise, so you don't try to eat them away. Release your emotions by stepping outside and going for a walk, writing in your journal, or calling a friend. Do anything that will make you feel better and help you regain some perspective.

Kirsten Binnie, Season 3, says, 'The Biggest Loser experience taught me that weight loss isn't just a physical process – it's also an emotional and mental journey. Losing weight requires you to be strong, both physically and in character. For most of us, losing weight will be a lifelong battle and you just have to stay on top of it. If you can manage your food and exercise at the same time, you are three quarters of the way there, and if you can add a support base on top of that and just keep going, day in and day out, that really is the secret to succeeding. There are challenges along the way and it's important not to give up. It is a long journey and you have to keep taking small steps every day.'

BIGGEST LOSER BIG TIP

The reality is it's going to be hard and there will be moments when you wonder if all the effort is worth it. The answer is 'Yes!' You deserve great things and you have to keep on moving forward.

Pati Singe, Season 2

SHANNAN SAYS

Michelle and I went away to Bali at the end of the last series and even then we trained every day and did workouts in the gym together. Neither Michelle nor I are blessed with freaky genetics and we have to work really hard to maintain our bodies. We constantly have to monitor what we eat and ensure we train most days of the week.

Do What the Experts Do

Michelangelo said, 'If people knew how hard I work to gain my mastery, it would not seem so wonderful at all.'

Excellence is not a one-off act. It is a way of living, an accumulation of small efforts repeated daily. To be a fit and healthy person you need to do the things fit and healthy people do. It means being dedicated to your new way of living and being healthy from your core.

'I definitely think like a fit person now,' says Garry Guerreiro, Season 3. 'I never want to put the weight back on, so I hold myself accountable for the choices I make. I need to keep thinking and living like a fit person would. If I decide to indulge in some takeaway, I choose Thai over fish and chips, and I won't let myself off the hook so easily these days. In the past if I forgot to pack a pair of socks for the gym then that would be it, but now I think, "You can get away with wearing the socks you have on, for one day." You need to ask yourself the tough questions – "Why am I avoiding the gym?" and "Why am I eating what I am eating?" – because all these factors add up. You need to be honest and constantly make the healthy choices.'

BIGGEST LOSER BIG TIP

You have to really push yourself out of your comfort zone because that is when you discover your strengths. If you keep staying in that little place where you feel comfortable you'll never learn the true extent of your capabilities. We often have no idea how strong we really are – mentally and physically. The focus is on 'I can't' rather than 'I can'. You have tell yourself 'I can do this!' every single day.

Alison Braun, Season 3

Trainer Shannan Ponton says, 'Even after 18 years in the fitness industry I still train each day and continually set myself goals. This year I aimed to run 12 kilometres in less than 48 minutes, which is really quick, and I did it. I also completed a 100-kilometre, 24-hour run through the bush, which was amazing. I've always got that little fire burning inside of me – I love to push myself and try new things. It's what motivates and inspires me.'

Trainers Shannan Ponton and Michelle Bridges stress that *The Biggest Loser* experience is not a temporary fix, but a way of life. Exercise and healthy eating are not just optional add-ons: they are the foundation of your physical, emotional and mental wellbeing.

'Exercise is my number-one priority every morning,' says Michelle. 'As a professional trainer, it's something I absolutely have to do for my career, of course, but I also adhere to the same principle when I have time off or I'm on holidays. If you want to get in shape and stay that way, you need to make sure you prioritise your health and do your exercise as early as you can each day. It always goes back to the same question: "What is your priority, and how badly do you want it?" '

Shannan agrees: '*The Biggest Loser* program is a complete lifestyle change – for life! The second you start to introduce excess calories or reduce your physical activity, you start to drift backwards. You have to maintain a healthy lifestyle every single day.

The most important shift you can make is to ditch the "victim" mentality. Be empowered, be strong and aim for success!'

Make Healthy Living a Family Affair

A great way to maintain your fantastic new way of living is to get the rest of the family involved. Now you have more energy, you can enjoy long walks, games in the park, hiking, going to the beach – you name it!

By exercising as a family, not only will you enjoy the benefits of your new way of life, but you will also see the positive effects on your loved ones.

Alison Braun, Season 3, says, 'It means so much that I can now run around with my kids. The benefits of my *Biggest Loser* experience have definitely flowed on to my family. My husband now joins me at the gym and my kids recognise the importance of keeping a healthy mind, soul and body. I can do so much more since I lost the weight – I race the kids to the park and go to the beach and join them on bike rides.

We spend a lot more time together as a family and everything now is so much more fun.'

Tracy Moores, Season 1, is in the same boat. 'I now feel I am in a much better position to empower my daughter and allow her to make healthy and informed lifestyle choices,' she comments. 'Leading by example is so important and creating the right environment for your family is imperative. Kids watch what you do rather than listen to what you say. By being healthy and active yourself there's a better chance the rest of your family will be healthy too.'

Alison and the Mountain

It never really occurred to me how much I had been missing out on life until we went to Hawaii and were given the challenge of climbing up a mountain.

There was a gate we had to go through for every week we had been in the house and at each gate we were given weights to replace the kilograms we had lost. By that stage I had lost 35 kilograms so I was looking forward to putting that many weights in my backpack and feeling the difference between what I used to feel and the way I had become. At first I was skipping along and had a real bounce in my step, knowing it was going to feel completely different.

The further I went along, though, and the more weight I accumulated in my backpack, the more depressed I felt. I hadn't anticipated the way all the old feelings of despair would come flooding back.

Suddenly I was thinking, 'I can't do this. That part is too steep so I'll have to walk around the side then go up.' It took me back to a time when I had to avoid stairs or certain paths because I physically wasn't able to deal with them.

As I trekked up the mountain all the old emotions came flooding back. By the time I got to the top I was in tears. This is what my life had been like all the time – the lack of strength, the embarrassment, the way I was incapable of doing everyday things that most people took for granted.

But then the backpack was taken away and it felt amazing. I felt so light, like I could fly. As I got to the top of the mountain I vowed never to go back. To this day I am still at the same weight I was when I left the house.

Alison Braun, Season 3.

Embrace Your New Life

As every Biggest Loser knows, weight loss entails a lot more than the physical effort of shedding kilograms. It also requires a great deal of internal strength, self-examination and having the courage to strip back the layers and allow the 'real you' to shine through. In many instances, other aspects of your life – apart from your weight – also change.

Alison Braun, Series 3, agrees. 'My life is so different now. I'm not just existing like I did before, I'm really living! In my old life before I lost the weight I constantly felt limited. I always used to tell my kids, "You can be anyone you want to be and you can do anything you want to do," but the truth is I wasn't living that life for myself. Now for the first time they have an empowered mum who is embracing life and showing them anything IS possible.'

BIGGEST LOSER BIG TIP

After you lose the weight, life becomes different in every way imaginable. I now live an enthusiastic life and a full life. I wake up each morning and know there is nothing holding me back.

Adro Sarnelli, Season 1

Strangely, many Biggest Losers feel that by losing weight and becoming smaller, they actually become more 'visible', which leads to greater feelings of confidence.

That was definitely the case with Garry Guerreiro, Season 3, who says, 'When I was overweight if I met a nice girl I'd think, "Why bother?", as I knew she wouldn't want to take me home to meet her parents. I could imagine them saying "What are you doing with that big guy?"

'Now I feel liberated, relaxed and confident and for the first time in ages people actually start making conversations with me. It was like I was invisible before but now I have my life and identity back. I have started to do things I have always wanted to do but in the past was too ashamed even to try.

'Recently I competed in the City to Surf, which is a 14-kilometre run, as well as running up the stairs of Centrepoint Tower. I ran 15,000 steps in 20 minutes.

That amazes me – I never believed I would be able to do things like that. I love to get out and do different things!'

In many ways, excess weight can serve as a protective barrier between you and the rest of society. Sharif Deen, Season 4, says that when you eradicate the layers you begin to feel a greater sense of freedom than ever before. 'You carry a lot of self-doubt when you're overweight. You create mental hurdles for yourself and you begin to think things will never get any better, that this is it. *The Biggest Loser* illustrated that I do have what it takes, and that if you push through the adversity and pain you'll come out the other side.'

Sharif's workmate, Teresa Hamilton, agrees. 'Ultimately, *The Biggest Loser* teaches us that we are in control. I am responsible for the way I act and the life I create for myself. It's empowering knowing that the only person I need to impress is me!'

Losing weight is an emotional journey that calls for courage, persistence, determination and strength. It is about realising your worth, and putting in the effort to be your best. Being healthy is a daily decision that you have to make and KEEP making. If there is one secret behind *The Biggest Loser* phenomenon, it is learning to take responsibility for yourself, your health and your life. It is about making that first vital decision to change and then moving towards your goals every single day.

By using *The Biggest Loser* success strategies, not only will you shed kilos, but you will also enjoy greater levels of energy, increased feelings of confidence, a stronger sense of self and a leaner physique. You can live the life you have always imagined.

Regardless of where you are now, lasting change is possible. It doesn't matter how many setbacks you have endured in the past, you are capable of creating a new exciting destiny for yourself – starting today!

Thank you to the fantastic people who made this book possible:

Jill Brown, the most incredible publisher in the universe; all those at FremantleMedia – Prue Mann, Valentina Gioia, Louise Restuccia, Marietta Delvecchio and David Berman; Kay Bently at A1 Transcriptions; Bradley Trevor Greive for guidance and support; Kerry Waters for providing research material; Anna Watkins for her superb editorial coordination; Ingo Voss for his gorgeous design; Nikla Martin for her outstanding production skills; and Elizabeth Cowell, Jessica Dettmann and Vanessa Battersby for their brilliant editorial work. Thanks also to *The Biggest Loser* trainers Michelle Bridges and Shannan Ponton and the contestants who had the courage to change their lives, and share their journey and heart.

Vanessa Waters

VANESSA WATERS is an award-winning Australian writer with over 15 years' experience in newspaper and magazine publishing. Residing in various natural locales, she is passionate about the ocean and staying true. Vanessa is inspired by all those who are brave enough to live their dreams.

An Ebury Press book
Published by Random House Australia Pty Ltd
Level 3, 100 Pacific Highway, North Sydney NSW 2060
www.randomhouse.com.au

First published by Ebury Press in 2009

Text copyright © Random House Australia, 2009
Photographs copyright © FremantleMedia 2009

The moral right of the author has been asserted.

Addresses for companies within the Random House Group can be found at www.randomhouse.com.au/offices

THE BIGGEST LOSER is a trademark of Reveille LLC and operated under licence by FremantleMedia Australia Pty Limited.

THE BIGGEST LOSER is produced by FremantleMedia Australia Pty Limited in association with Reveille LLC. www.fremantlemedia.com

Cover and internal design by VossDesign
Printed and bound in China by 1010 Printing International Ltd.

National Library of Australia
Cataloguing-in-Publication Entry

Waters, Vanessa.

Secrets of our success.

ISBN 978 1 74166 851 3 (pbk).

Biggest loser (Television program)
Reducing exercises.
Reducing diets.
Nutrition.
Motivation (Psychology)

613.712

Random House Australia uses papers that are natural, renewable and recyclable products and made from wood grown in sustainable forests. The logging and manufacturing processes are expected to conform to the environmental regulations of the country of origin.

10 9 8 7 6 5 4 3 2 1